iPad
for Beginners™

Imagine Publishing Ltd
Richmond House
33 Richmond Hill
Bournemouth
Dorset BH2 6EZ
☎ +44 (0) 1202 586200
Website: www.imagine-publishing.co.uk
Twitter: @Books_Imagine
Facebook: www.facebook.com/ImagineBookazines

Editor in Chief
Aaron Asadi

Production Editor
Amy Squibb

Senior Art Editor
Danielle Dixon

Printed by
William Gibbons, 26 Planetary Road, Willenhall, West Midlands, WV13 3XT

Distributed in the UK & Eire by
Imagine Publishing Ltd, www.imagineshop.co.uk. Tel 01202 586200

Distributed in Australia by
Gordon & Gotch, Equinox Centre, 18 Rodborough Road, Frenchs Forest,
NSW 2086. Tel + 61 2 9972 8800

Distributed in the Rest of the World by
Marketforce, Blue Fin Building, 110 Southwark Street, London, SE1 0SU.

iPad for Beginners © 2012 Imagine Publishing Ltd

ISBN 978 1908222664

IMAGINE
PUBLISHING

Contents

Welcome to
iPad
for Beginners™

The iPad is certainly one of the most intriguing products to have been released in recent times, and the excitement surrounding it is not unfounded. Allowing you to have extreme portability while still being able to do an incredible amount of day-to-day tasks, the iPad acts as a movable media hub, games console and much more, all alongside one of the most user-friendly and dynamic interfaces seen in a long time. It potentially changes the way we have being going about our lives for the last few years. Once you have your eager hands on this revolutionary device, you now need to find your way around it, and that can take a little getting used to. From using email, downloading apps and syncing with iCloud, all the way to using word processing and taking photos, **iPad for Beginners** ditches the jargon and shows you everything you need to know to set up your iPad and get started. Through easy to follow, step-by-step tutorials and features, we'll show you how to make the most out of this incredible piece of hardware, as well as pointing you in the direction of the essential apps you should download straight away. Welcome to the new wave of technology. Let's get started.

Find your way around the iPad hardware on page 8

146 Feature
100 essential apps
The must-have apps you simply have to download today

Introduction

Wi-Fi signal strength
This symbol lets you know the signal strength it is receiving

Available with or without 3G
If you want to use your iPad away from a Wi-Fi signal, you'll need the 3G model

16, 32 or 64GB
The iPad comes in various storage sizes – the 16GB is cheapest

10:15
Thursday, January 13

iPad

First look at the iPad

Let's explore the iPad's basic features

The iPad is unlike any computer you've ever put your hands on. For one thing, there's no intermediary between you and what you're trying to do; on a regular computer, you have to learn to manipulate a pointing device like a mouse or trackpad to move a cursor on the screen so you can achieve what you need to do. On the iPad, you're already an expert manipulator since you just use your fingers directly on the screen to move and affect what you see. If you know how to point, you know how to use an iPad, and that's the truly

exciting thing about this device: it makes personal computing truly personal.

But despite its obvious friendliness, it's still a remarkably complex piece of hardware and you'll need to know a little about what makes the iPad tick: how you turn it on, for instance, what's the function of its few buttons, and what about all the other controls embedded in the software itself? How can you use its many features to the fullest?

We will endeavour to show you all this over the next few pages, helping you feel comfortable with the device so you can hit the ground running in no time at all.

The volume control
Quickly control your sound with the buttons on the right

Battery level indicator
You can visually see how much power your iPad has left here

The Side Switch
Go to Settings to set this switch to either lock the screen rotation or instantly mute the sound

The on/off switch
Turn your iPad on or off by holding the top-right button

The screen (9.7" diagonal, with a resolution of 1024 x 768)
The iPad's high-res, LED-backlit screen is certainly impressive graphically for a tablet

The speaker grille
The speaker is located here, and it does a great job for a small device

The home button
This button takes you to the previous app launch screen.

The dock connector to sync and/or recharge
This is where you plug in your lead to sync or charge the iPad

Browsing

As soon as you've connected to your local wireless network, the iPad is ready to be an internet browsing device. In fact, when Apple's engineers were first experimenting with touchscreen devices, the original idea was a tablet designed for web browsing. As a result, going online is a very polished experience and a joy to use. Like all other applications on the iPad, tapping on the Safari icon fills the screen with that program's content, removing any other distractions from view. You can then browse the web with your fingers. If you're familiar with Safari on your Mac or PC, you'll feel right at home – there's even a Google search field, top right of the screen. Tapping on it increases its size and reveals the keyboard so you can type what you're looking for. The same applies for the address field if you know exactly where you want to go.

Thanks to iCloud, you can sync your Mac's bookmarks straight to your iPad, right down to the Bookmark Bar.

Navigating a webpage is easy; you flick your finger up, down, left or right to see other parts of the page. If you want to focus on a specific section, double-tap on it for it to zoom in and fill the screen.

There are other browsers on the App Store, such as Opera Mini and Atomic, so have a look to see if one suits your needs better than Safari.

Communication

Browsing the web isn't the only thing you need to do online. For one thing, you need to check your emails and the iPad's got you covered there as well, thanks to the Mail application. With it, you can setup as many accounts as you need. Just like Mail on your Mac, you have a universal inbox where all your messages, irrespective of which address they were sent to, can be accessed, read and replied to. You can also organise your messages in threads, making it easier to keep track of a conversation over time.

When it comes to social networking, you can either make use of Safari – aside from its games, Facebook works very well in the iPad's web browser (the games don't work because they rely on

Introduction

Adobe's Flash platform, which isn't compatible with the iPad, iPhone or iPod touch) – or look for the dedicated iPad apps, like Facebook and Twitter at the App Store. The latter has even been integrated into iOS 5 so that you can tweet from within a host of default Apple apps.

Other applications, like Skype, are also available, meaning you can enjoy full screen video calls on your iPad 2 with other people who don't necessarily own an Apple device, or there's the default FaceTime app for people who do.

Photos

If you see images on the web you'd like to keep, you can easily save them to your Photos application by tapping and holding on one and choosing 'Save Image' from the popover menu. But that's not the only use of that particular program. Thanks iOS 5's iCloud feature, you can activate Photo Stream so that any pictures taken on your iPad 2 or iPhone are automatically pushed to all of your iOS 5 devices and Macs running OS X 10.7.2 or higher.

You can also dispense with a bigger computer entirely by getting the iPad Camera Connection Kit and transfer photos and videos from any compatible digital stills camera straight to your iPad library – after which Photo Stream will make them instantly available on all of your devices, automatically and completely wirelessly.

Once there, you can browse through them, post them online or send them via email to friends and family. If you want to upload them to Facebook or Flickr for example, you can do this straight from their own dedicated applications, which you can download for free from the App Store.

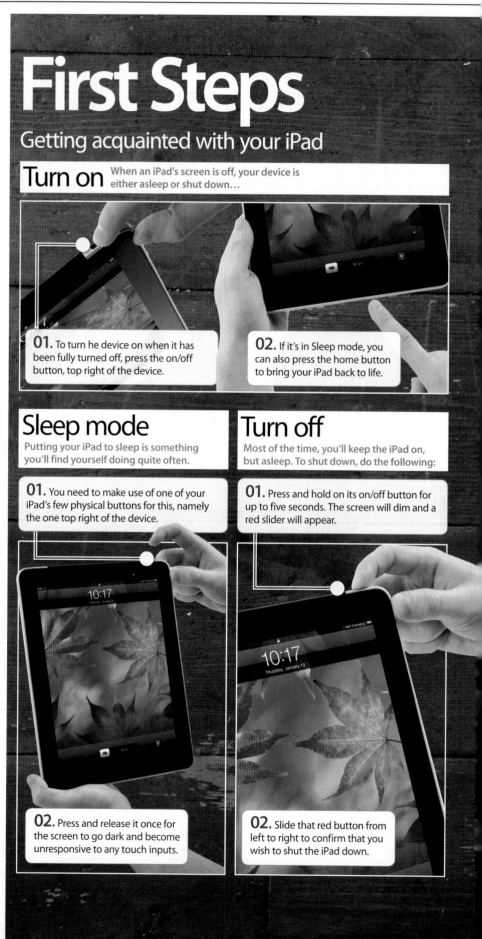

First Steps

Getting acquainted with your iPad

Turn on
When an iPad's screen is off, your device is either asleep or shut down…

01. To turn he device on when it has been fully turned off, press the on/off button, top right of the device.

02. If it's in Sleep mode, you can also press the home button to bring your iPad back to life.

Sleep mode
Putting your iPad to sleep is something you'll find yourself doing quite often.

01. You need to make use of one of your iPad's few physical buttons for this, namely the one top right of the device.

02. Press and release it once for the screen to go dark and become unresponsive to any touch inputs.

Turn off
Most of the time, you'll keep the iPad on, but asleep. To shut down, do the following:

01. Press and hold on its on/off button for up to five seconds. The screen will dim and a red slider will appear.

02. Slide that red button from left to right to confirm that you wish to shut the iPad down.

Change volume

Depending on what you're doing, you can change the volume is various ways...

01. Use the physical buttons, top of the iPad's right edge. The top one increases the volume and the bottom one lowers it.

02. If you're watching a movie or listen to music, you'll find a slider on the screen to achieve the same result.

Mute

To mute the volume, you have two options based on the iPad's physical buttons:

01. If you have the Side Switch set to Mute, slide it down to mute your iPad.

02. You can also press and hold the volume down button. After a couple of seconds, your iPad will be muted.

Rotation lock

You may wish to stop the screen from rotating each time you change position. Here's how:

01. Go to Settings and, under General there set the 'Use Side Switch to:' option to Lock Rotation and then slide the Side Switch.

02. If your Side Switch is set to Mute, double-tap the Home button, scroll to the right and then tap the lock button.

Charging

Recharging the iPad is a simple matter:

01. Unless your computer is recent enough, there won't be enough power from its USB port to charge the iPad.

02. For a faster, more efficient charge, it's best to use the bundled power adapter instead.

Brightness

If the screen is too light or dark for your tastes, you can alter it in a couple of ways:

01. Tap on the Settings app and select the 'Brightness & Wallpaper' menu. Use the slider to lower or raise the brightness.

02. Double-click the home button and slide the new bar of icons to the right. You'll find a brightness slider there as well.

Unlock

Once you've woken your iPad up, you'll be graced with its Lock Screen. What next?

01. To gain access to your device, use the slider at the bottom to unlock your screen.

02. If you have set a password, you'll have to type it in before you can proceed any further.

Syncing

To back up or transfer files, you need to sync...

01. Use the bundled cable to connect your iPad via one of your computer's USB ports.

Sync with iCloud Go to page 30 for this syncing option

02. It will launch iTunes and the backup and syncing process will by default be totally automatic.

Introduction

Music

It wouldn't be an Apple device if it didn't let you listen to your music, but although iTunes is responsible for almost everything media-related on your Mac, the iPad has broken those features into multiple applications designed for specific purposes. For instance, you can purchase new music using the iTunes application, but if you want to listen to albums you currently own, then you have to use the Music (formerly iPod) app. From there, you gain access to your songs, podcasts and audiobooks. If you want to watch a music video however, you'll need to take a trip to the Videos application.

But iTunes isn't the only way you can listen to music on your iPad. There are other programs that let you stream songs directly from the internet and just like the Music application, they can be used to listen to music in the background while you work in another program on your iPad. If you're in the UK, make sure you check out Spotify, while US readers should take a look at Pandora.

Watching

Although it's no substitute for your widescreen television, when you're away from your couch, the iPad makes for a surprisingly good TV. Due to its size, it's much better than an iPhone or iPod touch and its built-in speaker is good enough to allow the device to be shared, but what can you watch on it? Well, anything you've bought or rented from the iTunes Store will work on your iPad: you can transfer movies, TV shows, podcasts and music videos and they'll all play flawlessly on your portable device.

"Videos all play flawlessly on your portable device"

You could also convert your existing DVD collection into iTunes-compatible files but in order to achieve this, you'd need programs like HandBrake which are designed to transform your films and episodes into compatible files ready for you to enjoy on your iPad. This can be a time-consuming process, so if you'd rather not have to deal with any of this and you happen to own an Elgato Netstream device which is connected to your network, you can purchase the EyeTV application and watch live TV straight from your iPad, anywhere in your house, as long as you're within range of your wireless signal.

Entertainment

There's been a lot of talk about the iPad (and any other iOS device) not being compatible with Adobe's Flash, but this is actually less of a problem than you might think. For one thing, although you won't be able to go to www.youtube.com and watch videos via the Safari web browser, there's a dedicated YouTube application which enables you to do just that. You can watch clips, comment on them, and do pretty much everything you'd expect. Other video-sharing sites, like Vimeo, are getting on the iOS-friendly bandwagon and offer iPad-compatible versions of their videos, so you can watch those straight from your web browser.

But being entertained is much more than just passively watching something on the screen; you can also use your iPad to read the latest bestseller or enjoy a timeless classic. The two major programs that allow you to do this are Apple's own iBooks and Amazon's Kindle. Both are also compatible with the iPod and iPhone so you can stop reading on the iPad and carry on with another device if you'd like. That compatibility doesn't extend to your Mac for the iBooks though, but it does for the Kindle. Not all titles are available in digital form yet, but there's enough there to keep you busy for a long time.

Games

When it comes to games, you'll be spoilt for choice. There are so many available to download, both free or paid-for, so you can spend hours getting immersed in an adventure story (thank goodness for the iPad's excellent battery life), or just use it to while away a few minutes of your time.

The obvious choices are there, like arcade-type games such as *The Incident* and *Fruit Ninja HD*, to adventure games like *Hero of Sparta 2* and *Max*, to strategy games like *Cut the Rope* and *Angry Birds* or role-playing adventures like *Aralon* or *Galaxy on Fire 2*. There's even a version of *Farmville*.

But none of these offer anything new from what you could achieve on a regular computer. What sets the iPad apart from other platforms is that its screen is large enough that it can be easily viewed by multiple people at the same time. As a result, it's become a natural digital alternative to board games, making playing on a computer a much more social experience with people in the same room as you, just like the good old days. Make sure you check out titles like WarChess, Carcassonne, Scrabble, Monopoly and the Game of Life. Whatever your tastes, though, the iPad has it covered.

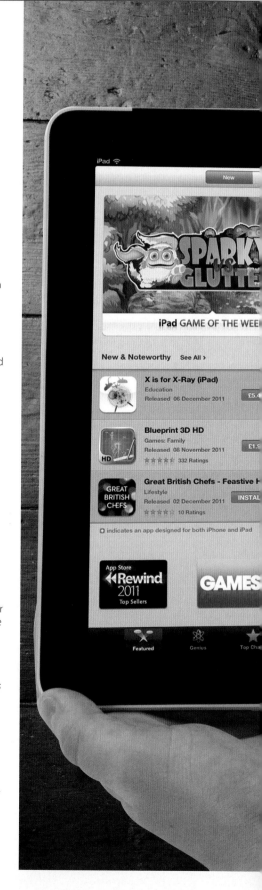

iTunes

The desktop software explored

What is iTunes?

A It's a program designed by Apple and the original purpose was to transfer your CD collection onto your Mac, catalogue your songs and transfer them to a compatible MP3 player. A lot's changed since these humble days.

Why do I need it?

A Because iTunes evolved over the years to accommodate more than music – from movies, TV shows, podcasts and more. Now it's the most popular way to transfer anything to your iPad.

Why is it not included on a CD?

A Apple now assumes that broadband is ubiquitous and that way, the company can make sure that you'll be using the very latest version available as opposed to one that could have been released months previously.

How do I cancel the sync?

A When your iPad is connected to iTunes, its screen informs you not to disconnect it from your computer. However, there's a slider at the bottom which you can use to cancel the sync should you need to. Your iPad will not be fully backed up if you do this, however.

Is there anything else I need -to do?

A Not really. The process is completely automatic and if you don't want to get any more involved in the process, you don't have to. Once the sync is complete, you can unplug your device and carry on using it.

Can I control what's on my iPad?

A Absolutely. Look down iTunes' sidebar until you find the Devices section. Click on your iPad and the main part of the interface will let you choose

Where can I get it?

A Point your browser towards *www.itunes.com* and click on the 'Download iTunes' button, somewhere on the page (it's currently on the right, near the top, but that could change).

It's installed. Now what?

A Double-click on its icon to open it and agree to the licence agreement. You can convert your music CDs to iPad-compatible files or purchase new songs, movies and shows from the iTunes Store. But none of this is compulsory.

What happens when I connect my iPad to my computer?

A iTunes will take over your iPad and you will be asked not to disconnect it while the syncing process is taking place. Your iPad's data will be backed up and your media will be synchronised between both devices.

which songs, films, podcasts, applications and so on you'd like to transfer over.

What about my emails, calendars and contacts?

A That's all possible as well from the same section in iTunes as mentioned above. You can find all the details and choose which calendars, contacts and emails you'd like to import from the Info section.

Introduction

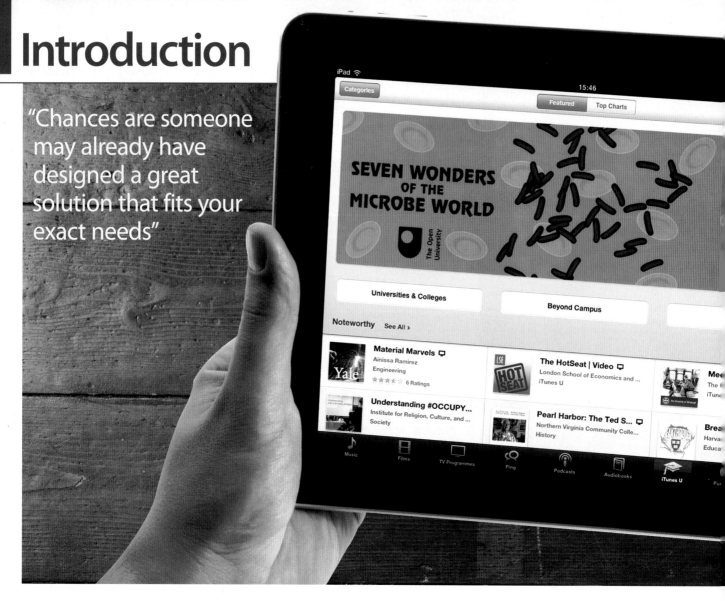

"Chances are someone may already have designed a great solution that fits your exact needs"

Office work

The iPad isn't just a device to browse the web, watch videos and play games however. Many people classify it as just a media consumption device, but it's in fact a very powerful machine capable of doing almost anything a regular computer can. It comes with a Notes program which you can use to jot down a few ideas, lists, or even the beginning of a draft letter. That application syncs with your emails and you can access those documents in your Mac's Mail program, which is very convenient and enables you to work between the two systems.

But the iPad can go a lot further than this. For one thing, the iWork suite is available for it as a separate purchase. You won't obviously get all the features you've grown accustomed to with the Mac's versions, but for a first attempt at creating a business suite that's controlled by touch, it's remarkable what you can do with them and you'll be designing newsletters, filling in spreadsheets and creating presentations in next to no time.

If you need compatibility with Microsoft Word and iWork's conversion layer isn't good enough, take a look at Byte^2's Office^2 HD. It's not as attractive as the iWork suite, but it lets you create native Word (both .doc and .docx) and Excel (.xls) documents on your iPad for a very reasonable price.

Productivity

As for other productivity programs, Calendar stores all your appointments and syncs with iCal on your Mac – as long as you have activated your free iOS 5 iCloud account. The same applies for the Contacts app, even preserving all your groups so you'll feel right at home on your new machine.

Surprisingly, unlike the iPod touch or iPhone, the iPad doesn't come with a calculator, but this can be easily remedied with a short visit to the App Store. Just type on "Calculator" in the search field to find enough free and paid options to satisfy your needs.

Another feature missing from the iPad is any possibility of using it like an external drive, but the fantastic advantage of the iPad and any device powered by the iOS software is the huge number of developers working on it. As a result, someone's come up with a way of achieving just that thanks to an application called 'USB Disk Pro for iPad' (a free version is also available under the title of 'USB Disk for iPad') so you can easily use your iPad like an external portable hard drive.

Chances are, whatever it is you're looking for, someone may already have designed a solution that fits your exact needs.

Creative apps

That's exactly the case with graphic design applications. Adobe, maker of the mighty Photoshop, has only dipped its toes in the iPad, but other, smaller developers have jumped at the opportunity that this new platform offers them and there's a wealth of programs that allow you to design with your fingers anything you used to need a mouse or a graphic tablet for in the past.

App Store FAQ

A vital part of the iPad explained

What's all this talk about apps? Do I need them?

A Apps, or applications, are programs that run on a computer, like your browser or word processor. They increase your device's functionality and you should definitely browse through them to see if there's anything you might find crucial to your life on the iPad.

Where do I get those apps?

A Straight from the App Store, which you can access from iTunes or the iPad app. You might find some websites showcasing various programs, but you can only get them from the App Store.

What if I'm just browsing? Can I find stuff easily?

A Of course: the App Store is really designed to help you buy programs. As a result, you can look through various lists like top sellers, top free apps, staff recommendations, and so on.

Is there any trial software I can use?

A Not as such, but many developers have 'lite' or 'free' versions of their applications. These offer limited functionality or a few sample levels if it's a game. If you like what you see, you can then purchase the full program and delete the lite copy.

How do I find what I want?

A With over 60,000 apps designed specifically for the iPad, you may feel that you may never find the exact program you need. Try using the search field to narrow down the results.

Can I only get them from my computer?

A No: there's a program called 'App Store' on your iPad. From there, you can gain access to the entire store as well, although you will need to be within range of a Wi-Fi network, unless of course you own an 3G-capable iPad.

It's all a bit of a jumble; can I narrow my search down?

A The App Store is broken into 20 categories, each with its own top sellers list. You can narrow your search by focusing on a single category.

Why can't I comment on a program I'm looking at?

A In order to limit bogus reviews or overly negative or positive comments from people who've never used the program, Apple links your reviews to your account. The company can therefore check if you own the app and if you don't, you can only read, not contribute.

How can I ask questions or get help from the developer?

A At the bottom of every app description is a link to the developer's own website. More often than not, you'll find a help forum or contact email address there which you can use to write to the developer or company and get the help you need.

Why does my App Store icon have red numbers on it?

A These badges are there to show you that some of the programs you've acquired have been updated and that you can get those new versions for free directly from the App Store's Updates section on your iPad (or computer).

> "The iPad is a very powerful machine capable of doing almost anything a computer can"

The beauty of the iPad is that these programs are so cheap compared to those you'd find on a Mac or PC, that trying some out isn't as financially crippling as it can be on other platforms.

You're bound to find the right program that matches your abilities. If you're professionally inclined, have a look at SketchBook Pro, Freeform or Brushes. If you're looking for programs that help you transform pictures into visually stunning works of art, explore Artist's Touch or the PhotoArtistaHD series of applications. If you fancy more specific effects, consider TypeDrawing or Glow Painter Pro HD. Those of you missing iPhoto's adjustment tools should purchase TouchUp, and your children (or the child inside you) will love Drawing Pad.

Kids

The iPad is an amazing learning tool no matter what your age is; there's even a dedicated section called "Apps for Kids" in the App Store where you can get interactive books like *Winnie the Pooh* or *The Cat in the Hat*, programs that teach you how to read and write or even understand the world around you, help you play music, draw, … pretty much anything you can imagine.

Older children haven't been left out either: MathBoard is a fantastic program designed to help you perfect your algebra. You can even set which calculations to work on and how difficult they should be. There are also things to keep them entertained such as wordsearch apps like WordSeek HD and much more.

If you're interested in space, you can learn everything you need to know thanks to programs like Solar Walk or Solar System for iPad, and the little ones can keep up with their older siblings with iLearn Solar System HD. If it's dinosaurs you're after, check out Ultimate Dinopedia, and if you want to explore all the elements that make up our universe, be sure to look for The Elements - there's even a British edition with UK English spelling.

Maps

All of the above can be achieved whether you own a Wi-Fi only-iPad or one capable to connecting to a 3G network (ie, one that hooks up to a mobile phone network and hence gets you online wherever you have coverage – for a price). If you've decided to invest in a 3G-capable iPad, the capabilities of your machine are greatly extended since you'll be able to browse, check you emails or even play online games wherever you might be.

There's also the added advantage of being able to use the Maps application to help you navigate to your desired location. This application will even show you areas to avoid due to traffic jams or dense circulation. But even if you decided to stick to the Wi-Fi-only version, you should definitely give Maps a try. You may get tired of hearing how "magical" the iPad is, but it's undeniable how truly amazing it is to be able to scroll through a map and effortlessly zoom in and out of a location using your fingers alone. The program is incredibly responsive and the only limitation you'll experience will be due to your internet's bandwidth. It illustrates just how wonderful using this device truly is. There are also other map apps available, so check out the App Store to find one that suits you.

Accessories

Enrich your hardware with some great kit…

Keyboard The iPad is great for many things, although some people still struggle with typing using the device. You can get around this by purchasing an Apple Wireless Keyboard and then pairing it with your iPad via Bluetooth

Smartcase This device will enthral you for hours with its ingenuity. With the clever use of magnets you can, literally, sling this cover at your iPad 2 and it will auto-align to sit perfectly across the screen of your device for supreme protection. What's more, when you pull it back, your device will automatically wake up

Case Getting an iPad case is essential if you wish to protect your investment and they come in many styles. Most can display your iPad in portrait or landscape orientations and can be supported at a variety of angles for browsing, working or watching movies

Protective films
Even if you prefer your iPad to be without a case, you should consider a film around its most important part: the screen. Some high quality ones not only protect it from accidental scratches, they actually make it easier to clean and fingerprints don't stick as easily as they would on a bare piece of glass

Speakers The iPad's mono speaker may be surprisingly good for an item of its size, but it's really not sufficient to enjoy your media to its fullest. Thankfully, there are many external speakers available to improve the experience. They either connect via its mini-jack, the dock connector or even wirelessly via Bluetooth

Apple TV Your iPad is a great device to play all of your downloaded movies, videos and music, but if you want to broadcast them on a bigger stage then Apple TV is perfect. This device transforms your TV into a viewing portal for all of your Apple content and it does so wirelessly – you just sit back and control your evening's entertainment from your iPad

Styluses Controlling objects with your fingers undoubtedly feels more natural, but a stylus can be great for precision work. A few companies have created such devices that work very well with the iPad's capacitive screen

Introduction

Everything you need to know about iOS 5

Find out how Apple's new mobile operating system is going to revolutionise the way you use your iPad

iCloud

iCloud is an online service that stores all of your content and wirelessly pushes it to all of your iOS-based device, Mac or PC. iCloud is automatically integrated with your apps, allowing new content to be pushed to the cloud and then shared with

other devices. All content, such as purchased music, books, photos, settings and app data will all be backed up over Wi-Fi and distributed to all devices, and Mail, Contacts and Calendars have all been reworked to accommodate iCloud's functionality,

which is free up to 5GB. The service also extends to documents from Apple's iWork productivity suite, which includes apps such as Pages, Numbers and Keynote to allow them to be synced and distributed to other devices quickly and easily.

RIGHT: iCloud will change the way to use your device.

"The service also extends to documents from Apple's iWork productivity suite"

iMessage

One of the most exciting features of iOS 5 is iMessage, which allows you to send text messages, photos, videos and contact information to anyone with an iDevice – across all platforms. This service works over Wi-Fi or 3G, supports group discussions and is integrated into Notification Center, making it impossible for you to miss a message.

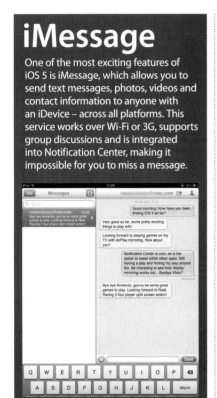

PC free!

Undoubtedly the most welcome feature of iOS 5 is wireless syncing. That's right, you no longer have to connect your iPad – or iPhone if you have one as well – to your PC, with actual cables. Now all syncing can be done exclusively on the device itself without having to tether it to your desktop machine, and that even includes syncing your entire iTunes library. Viva la revolution! This feature also brings over-the-air updates that contain only the data that's changed, meaning you don't have to re-download the entire OS every time subtle tweaks are made.

Photo Stream

An extension of iCloud, Photo Stream automatically uploads photos (either taken with or synced to iDevices) to the cloud and pushes them to other devices. If you take a picture on your iPhone, it will appear on your iPad or laptop. Photos are stored in your cloud for 30 days, and don't count towards your 5GB allowance.

"Take a picture on your iPhone and it'll appear on your iPad or laptop"

iTunes in the iCloud

Now onto the music. iTunes in the Cloud means that any purchased albums or individual tracks from iTunes can be stored in your cloud and redownloaded to other devices at no extra cost. Which is all well and good, but if you download them to iTunes then they can already be synced to other devices, right? Indeed, but there is an additional option you can toggle that will automatically download a copy of each track to other devices. Another intriguing feature of iTunes in the Cloud is iTunes Match. This scans your music library, and upgrades it to the 256Kbps AAC DRM-free files, as long as they are available in the iTunes store, ensuring that your collection boasts the best sound quality. This service comes at an annual fee of $25.

Safari Reader

When you access a website, you just want the cold, hard facts delivered to your eyes without the needless clutter that peppers pages, right? Apple thinks so too, which is why Safari Reader strips all of the clutter out of a webpage, giving you just the text without the excess content. This feature is accessible via a button next to the address bar, and while we're not sure what this feature means to the future of web advertisers, we like it.

Other notable features include a Reading List, which accumulates a list of pages to read offline later at your own leisure, plus tabbed webpages for quick and easy access without having to leave your current page and scroll through your list of open pages. Safari has been greatly enhanced by iOS 5.

Introduction

Quicker camera

When the iPad 2 was launched, the inclusion of a front- and rear-facing camera was welcomed with open arms. Not only did this mean FaceTime was possible, but people could also snap away when out and about with their iPad. However, the size of the iPad also made it difficult at times to tap the camera button on-screen to take an image. Thankfully, iOS 5 has brought with it the ability to take photos simply by pressing the volume up button in the Camera app. This means you can take pictures not only quicker, but in a much more comfortable way than before, meaning you'll never miss that perfect picture again.

Twitter integration

Heavily rumoured prior to the big announcement, iOS 5 integrates Twitter, with many apps such as Camera, Photos, Safari and Maps including the option to tweet from within. This also extends to Contacts, where you will be able to link your contacts and keep their information updated. You only sign into Twitter once, via Settings, and the information is shared among the apps that use it.

Notification Center

Accessible by swiping down a menu from the top of the screen, the Notification Center organises all of your app notifications into one easy-to-manage list. Every notification has an 'X' icon situated next to it for easy dismissal, and there is no escape from the notifications on your Lock screen either. By swiping across a message, you are taken directly into it, saving you the time and hassle of having to unlock your device first. You are also alerted no matter what app you're in.

Better Photos

The Photos app has been given a massive overhaul in iOS 5, and to many this is long-overdue. Photos will now feature some new in-app editing options, such as cropping, image rotation, auto-enhance and red-eye reduction. You can also organise your photos into albums on your device and, using iCloud, push them to all of your iOS devices – so if you're taking photos on your iPhone, iCloud will automatically send copies to your iPad.

"Photos will now feature some new in-app editing options, such as cropping and image rotation"

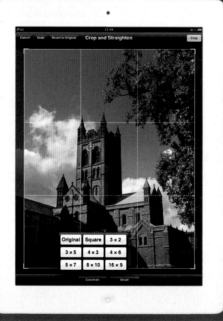

Reminders

For the absent-minded, there is no excuse to forget groceries at the supermarket or neglect to buy flowers for a loved one again with Reminders. This feature is synced to Calendar, and is location-based, which means the app will remind you to do things based on where you are thanks to a 'geo-fence' that will alert you when you leave or enter a certain location.

Newsstand

As app-based magazines become a more popular alternative to print-based publications, there is now an app that houses all of your magazine and newspaper subscriptions. Like iBooks, Newsstand lays out your media on virtual shelves for you to admire the eye-catching covers before delving into the publication proper. All new purchases go directly into your Newsstand folder, and as new issues become available, Newsstand automatically updates them in the background.

> ## "Newsstand lays out your media on shelves for you to admire"

Calendar enhancements

You can now get more perspective on your schedule with a year view on the iPad, so you know what the next 12 months hold. Tap to create an event and drag to adjust the time and duration. You can add, rename and delete calendars directly from your device, and view event attachments even without having to leave the app.

New Mail

Mail users will be delighted to learn that enhancements have been made to allow messages to be flagged or searched, text to be formatted, indents added, and names dragged into the address fields. A split-keyboard option also pushes half of the keyboard to either side of the screen, which will suit users who use their thumbs to type.

Extra Game Center features

A host of subtle tweaks have been added to make Game Center a more competitive battleground. With iOS 5, you can post a profile picture, get new friend recommendations based on the games you play and the gamers you already know, and you can discover new games without leaving the app. And that's not all – Apple has taken a leaf out of Microsoft's book by awarding you Achievement scores, giving you bragging rights over your mates.

New multitasking gestures

One of the more subtle new features of iOS 5 is a selection of new moves and shortcuts to help you get around your iPad even quicker. Using four or five fingers, you can swipe up to reveal the multitasking bar, pinch to return to the Home screen, and swipe in the left or right direction in order to switch between apps.

> ## "Swipe in the left or right direction to switch apps"

And there's more

So many exciting new features have been showcased, and we're not even at the end yet, because Apple has also announced new AirPlay Mirroring options for iPad, and additional accessibility features for users with mobility, hearing, vision and cognitive disabilities. With AirPlay, you can wirelessly stream whatever's on your iPad 2 to your HDTV via iPad 2, which should prove useful in the classroom.

Setting up

Bring your iPad to life with these easy to follow tips to get you up and running

24 Activate & register

28 Set up iCloud

34 Get to know iTunes

46 Customise your iPad

Setting up

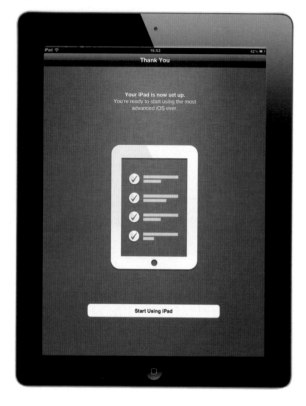

How to activate and register a new iPad

Just got an iPad? We guide you through the process of setting up your device and registering it to your Apple ID

With trembling hands and a giddy sensation in your stomach, you unpack your brand-new iPad from its box and are ready to activate it and start using it to enhance your life. But whereas previously you would have to have had a computer to plug your iPad into to start the setup process, with iOS 5 you no longer need to tether your device to a computer and the entire setup can be carried out independently, which makes it a quick and easy process.

All you have to do is connect your new device to a power source and then press the Sleep/Wake button, which is situated on the top of your iPad. This will bring up a generic iPad lock screen with a slider at the bottom. Tap and hold on the slider with your index finger and swipe it to the right to unlock the device and the next series of screens will guide you through the setup process. In this tutorial we will take you through each stage of the process and explain what each screen is asking you to do.

"All you have to do is connect your device to a power source and press a button"

Activation Prepare your iPad

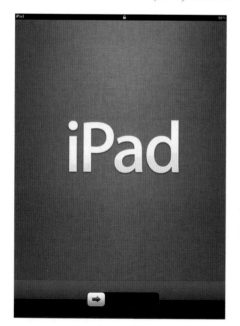

01 Unlock your device

When you first switch on your iPad you will be presented with a plain-looking lock screen with a slider at the bottom. Tap and hold the slider and swipe it to the right to unlock the iPad.

02 Select your language

You will be presented with a long list of different languages. The language you choose here will be the language that your device is set to and the language that all text will be presented in.

03 Select your Country or Region

Now select your Country or Region. This will determine the apps that are available in the App Store and the various media available from the iTunes app, as well as the correct currency.

Exploring your Home screen

Once your iPad has been set up, start exploring

Your apps
A selection of Apple apps are built into the operating system and will appear on your Home screen as standard. Tap on an icon to launch the app

Your Settings
Your first port of call should be the Settings app. Tap on this to start modifying and customising certain aspects of your device

Adding apps
The Dock contains four apps as standard but you can add an extra one by tapping and holding on an icon until it starts to shake and then dragging it with your finger into the Dock

Your Dock
The Dock is a row of app icons in a strip at the bottom of the screen. This Dock is present no matter which of your screens you're on and should be used for your most-used apps

Tweaking options
If you couldn't decide whether to activate certain services such as Find My iPad and iCloud during the initial setup process then you can do it later. Just tap on your Settings app and you will find the relevant options there to activate and start using these features.

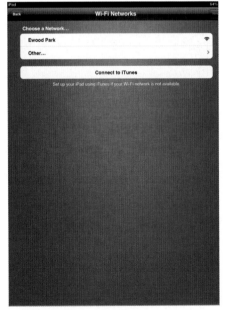

04 Location Services
The next part of the process is dedicated to your device's Location Services. This allows apps to gather and use data indicating your approximate location. This is useful if you lose your device.

05 Enable or disable
You can either enable or disable Location Services. If you are unsure of the purpose of this feature and need more information then don't worry; you can activate it later from Settings.

06 Connect to a network
Your iPad relies on a Wi-Fi network to be able to connect to the internet and fuel a wealth of different services. If you are within range of a Wi-Fi network then it will be detected.

Setting up

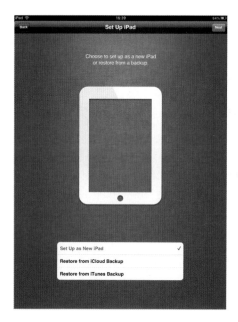

07 Set up iPad

The next screen presents you with three options. You can either set up the device as a new iPad, which is what you'll be doing, or restore it from previous settings backed up to iCloud or iTunes.

08 Sign in

You'll need your own Apple ID to enjoy the main features of your iPad, such as being able to download apps, music and media and back up and sync your data and settings with iCloud.

09 Enter Apple ID

If you have an Apple ID you can tap 'Sign In with an Apple ID' or create one by tapping the 'Create a Free Apple ID' option. If you choose the latter you will be guided through the creation process.

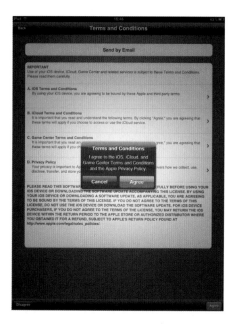

10 Read the T&Cs

After signing in, you will be presented with a screen of Terms and Conditions that relate to all aspects of your iPad and the services that you will be using, such as iCloud, Game Center, etc.

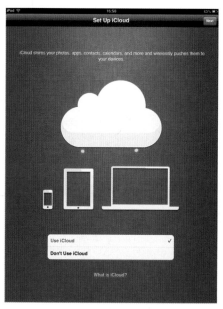

11 Set up iCloud

Apple's iCloud is new to iOS 5 and it allows you to back up data from your iPad to your own cloud storage space. Here you can opt in to the service; it won't cost you anything.

12 Find My iPad

If you misplace your iPad then Find My iPad will help you locate it on a map, play a sound or display a message. You can activate this service to sync the location of your device with your iCloud.

Exploring your Settings

Start personalising your iPad through Settings

The categories
All of the categories to which the Settings apply will be presented in a list on the left-hand side of the screen. Tap an option to bring up its individual screen of settings

Side Switch
The switch on the side of your device can be used for muting sound or locking your screen rotation. The latter is very useful and you can assign it from the 'General' Settings section

All about your iPad
By tapping on the 'About' option in the 'General' section, you can get in-depth info on your device, such as the serial number, capacity and the amount of space that your various apps and media take up

Software Update
By tapping on the 'Software Update' option in the 'General' section your device will be able to find and update your iOS, without the need to connect your device to a computer

Restoring from backup
You may not be setting up a brand new iPad; you may just be restoring your existing iPad using an iCloud backup. In which case the setup process is still carried out the same way, but when you're asked to set up your iPad, choose 'Restore from iCloud Backup' and all of your previous settings will be restored and all of your apps and media will be redownloaded – it may take a while though…

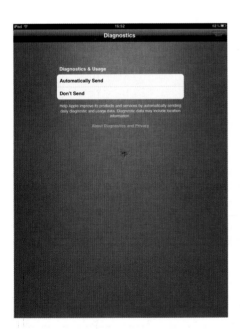

13 Diagnostics & Usage
Apple likes to keep track of how its products are performing, so this screen allows you to send diagnostic data straight to Apple. Opt for 'Don't Send' to keep your information private.

14 Set up complete
Congratulations! You have now worked your way through the entire set-up process. A screen will confirm the process is complete, so what are you waiting for? Tap on the 'Start Using iPad' button!

15 Start using your iPad
You'll be presented with your Home screen, so start tapping on icons to launch apps and find your way around, experimenting with the gestures needed to operate your new device.

Setting up

Set up an iCloud account

All of your documents can be moved wirelessly from device to device without you having to lift a finger

With iOS 5 came iCloud, a new service from Apple that is so much more than just a hard drive in the sky. Free to all iOS 5 users, iCloud automatically and securely stores your content so that it's always available on your iPad, iPhone, Mac… whatever device you're using. Through iCloud you get full access to your music, apps, photos and documents, and it also wirelessly syncs all of your emails, contacts and calendars to keep them up to date across all of your devices.

When you sign up for iCloud you get 5GB of free storage, which is plenty because all of your music, apps, books, and photos that are pushed to all of your devices don't count against your free storage. And seeing as your mail, documents, account info, settings and other app data don't use up much space, you'll find that your free quota goes a long way. You can now set up iCloud when you register, but if you opted not to or you registered your iPad before the iOS 5 update, follow these steps to set up iCloud now.

"When you sign up for iCloud you automatically get 5GB of free storage"

iCloud Setting up your personal iCloud

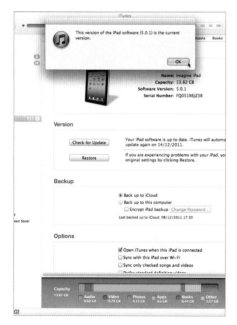

01 Update to iOS 5

iCloud comes as part of iOS 5, so connect your device to your computer through iTunes and check to ensure that you have the latest free software update installed on your device.

02 Launch Settings

There is very little tinkering to do to set up your iCloud. Start off by launching your Settings app, and in the column on the left-hand side of the screen will be a section called 'iCloud'. Tap on this.

03 Sign in

To activate your iCloud account you will need to log in using your Apple ID, which is the same email address and password that you use for your other services, such as iTunes and the App Store.

Your iCloud Settings

Activating your free iCloud account is simple and easy to manage

Your account
Your free iCloud is activated when you enter your Apple ID. This is the same email address and password that you use for other Apple services, like iTunes

Storage & Backup
You can select the option to automatically back up your iPad to iCloud under certain conditions and purchase more storage space if you need it

Compatible apps
iCloud is integrated into a host of default Apple apps and works behind the scenes to make sure everything is synced across all devices

Delete Account
If you are upgrading your device and wish to disassociate your current iPad with an iCloud account then simply tap the 'Delete Account' option

Documents in the Cloud
One of the best features of iCloud, Documents in the Cloud, enables you to work on Pages, Numbers or Keynote documents on your iPad and then, without the need to save or manually transfer them, your documents will automatically appear on your iPhone or Mac for you to work on later. Enable the 'Documents & Data' option in your iCloud Settings to make it so.

04 Merge data
If you've already set up an iCloud account on another device, then you will be asked if you'd like to merge data, such as calendars, with the data that exists on the iCloud. Choose 'Merge'.

05 Tailor your options
You can now start selecting which of the apps utilise the service. Move the sliders to activate the apps. Photo Stream, Documents & Data and Notes are disabled by default.

06 Automatic downloads
To get the most out of iCloud, click on the Store section in Settings and then turn on 'Automatic Downloads' for Music, Apps and Books to download all new purchases from other devices.

App used:
N/A

Time needed:
10 minutes

Sync your apps with iCloud

Your iCloud can work wonders behind the scenes to wirelessly move your documents between devices

 Now that you've learned a bit about iCloud and set up your free account, we'll teach you about how this fantastic service works in tandem with certain apps on your iPad.

There is no disputing that iCloud is a very useful service that can benefit you in myriad ways and make life significantly easier, but unless you know exactly how then there seems little point in activating your free account. For example, should you activate Photo Stream if you don't take any photos? And is it worth switching the Documents & Files feature on if you don't have any iWork apps on your Mac? In this tutorial we guide you through each of the app options that you are presented with on the iCloud Settings screen and describe what each feature does. From this you can decide if you need it on or not and go about utilising the ones that you do activate. But however you decide to use iCloud, before too long you'll wonder how you ever managed without it.

"iCloud is a very useful service that can benefit you in myriad ways"

iCloud Which apps should you activate?

01 Mail, Contacts & Calendars
If you lead a busy lifestyle and use multiple iOS 5 devices then you should enable all three of these options so that calendar events, contacts and emails are synced and updated.

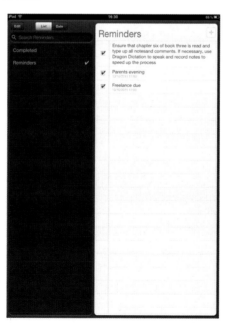

02 Reminders
Reminders is a new free app that lets you make 'to do' lists and set reminders. By activating it in iCloud then all of your devices will remind you, not just the one you set the reminder on.

03 Safari Bookmarks
Enabling Bookmarks ensures that all items stored in your Safari Reading List are also synced across devices, making it easy to start browsing on your iPhone and continue on your iPad.

Activate iCloud apps

Syncing apps to iCloud is as easy as moving sliders with your fingers

Your account
You can view your iCloud account information by tapping on the Account section at the top of the iCloud Settings screen

Enabling apps
To utilise the iCloud features of your apps, to sync info and data across devices, simply move the slider of each app to the 'On' position

Extra options?
The Photo Stream and Documents & Data options have extra screens. There are no additional options associated with them, just more detailed explanations

Storage used
You can see how much of your free five-gigabyte allocation is being used by clicking on the 'Storage & Backup' option

Piece of mind
If you mislay your iPad, then worry not. As long as you enable the 'Find My iPad' option on the iCloud Settings screen, the position of your device will be stored in your iCloud and can be accessed from any computer web browser by going to **www.icloud.com**.

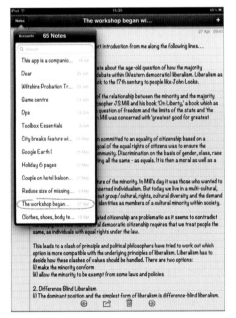

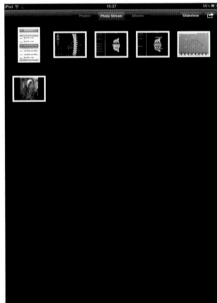

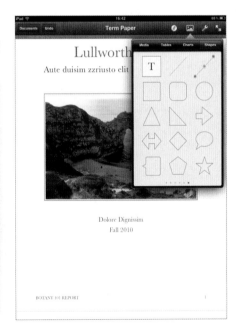

04 Notes
Moving the 'Notes' slider to the 'On' position will ensure that any notes that you make through the Notes app on one device will be synced and made available to read and edit on other devices.

05 Photo Stream
This is a brilliant feature that does away with the need to email images between devices. If you take a photo on your iPhone, with Photo Stream it will appear in Photos on your iPad in seconds.

06 Documents & Data
As long as you have the same iWork apps on your Mac or iPhone, this ensures any changes you make on your iPad will be reflected on your other devices, without needing to save or transfer.

Install iTunes on your desktop

 App used: iTunes

 Time needed: 15 minutes

Although you no longer need to connect your device to your computer in order to start using it and for getting system updates, installing iTunes on your computer is still a worthwhile exercise…

 Since the release of iOS 5, all Apple mobile devices, including your iPad, can be used straight out of the box without the need to connect it to a copy of iTunes – as was previously the case. But downloading and installing the latest copy of iTunes on your computer is still recommended as it allows you to perform a series of useful tasks.

Primarily, through iTunes you can still convert your CD collection to MP3 format and then copy the files to your iPad, but the latest version, OS X 10.5, also embraces Apple's iCloud service so that any music you purchase through iTunes – be it on your iPad or Mac – is automatically pushed to all of your devices wirelessly. What's more, through iTunes in the Cloud you can also access all of your previous iTunes purchases from any device and then redownload them for the current device at no extra cost. You can also connect your iPad to your computer via USB and perform app backup and syncing processes.

In this tutorial we guide you through the process of downloading and installing the latest version of iTunes.

"The iPad needs to hook up with iTunes before you can do anything else"

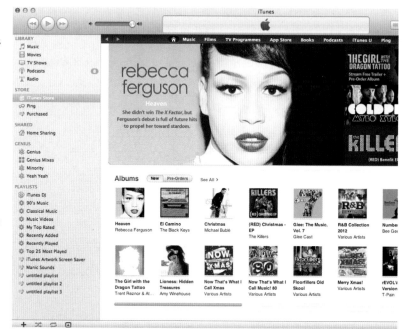

iTunes Installing iTunes on your Mac or PC

01 Get online

Your first step is to launch your favourite web browser and point it in the direction of www.itunes.com. The layout of the page changes regularly, but there will be a 'Download iTunes' button somewhere within it (currently, it's located in the top-right corner of the page).

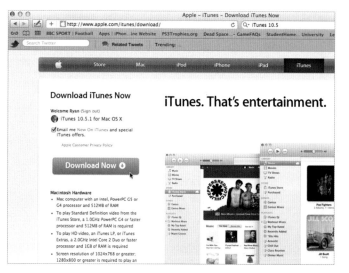

02 Download now

This will lead you to the proper download page. Your browser will recognise the type of computer you're on so you won't be offered any choices that could lead to confusion. You'll see a single 'Download Now' button. Only enter your email if you want to receive promotional messages from Apple.

The iTunes Download page

What each part of the Download page does

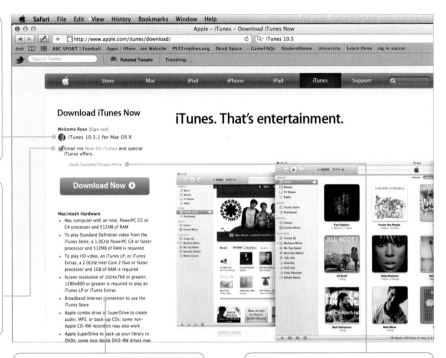

Automatic detection
All modern browsers transmit what type of computer you are currently using and clever websites can take advantage of that information to only offer you the choices that match those criteria

Email notifications
By default, these two tick boxes are enabled, which means that you won't be able to download iTunes without typing in your email address first. If you'd rather stay anonymous, untick them

System requirements
If you're at all uncertain if your computer will be able to run the software, this section displays the necessary system requirements that match the machine you're currently running

Privacy Policy
If you're concerned about what Apple might do with the information you give them (namely, your email address, as requested on this page), you can check out its policy by clicking here

What exactly is iTunes in the Cloud?
The iCloud is a free cloud storage services first introduced by Apple as part of the iOS 5/OS X 10.7.2 updates. iTunes takes advantage of this service with 'iTunes in the Cloud', a range of features that allow you to have access to your music collection more freely. iTunes now stores your music and TV purchases in your personal iCloud and makes them available on your device, anywhere, any time and at no additional cost. Furthermore, any music purchased from iTunes will pushed to your other devices, such as your Mac or iPhone automatically and wirelessly. And don't worry, all previously purchased music before the advent of iCloud won't be forgotten because you can redownload it all on any device.

03 Installing

Once the download is complete, a new window will open up with a semi-transparent iTunes logo inside it. The 'Read Before You Install iTunes' document gives you the minimum requirements without which the program will not function. Double-click 'Install iTunes' to proceed.

04 Licence Agreement

Once iTunes has been installed, its icon should appear in your Dock or Desktop. If it hasn't you'll be able to locate it in your Applications or Program Files folder. The first time you double-click on it, you'll have to agree to the licence agreement. Agreeing grants you access to the software.

Setting up

Get to know the iTunes interface

iTunes has morphed from a program designed to look after your music library to one capable of storing any media you'd care to enjoy, all while being the gateway to Apple's online store

The first version of iTunes was released over a decade ago, back on 9 January 2001. Apple had purchased Casady and Greene's SoundJam MP two years previously, realising that it had missed the boat with regards to the CD ripping and burning that was going on at the time. Back then, the iPod didn't even exist. Three years later, the iTunes Music Store was born, along with Apple's ambitions as an online entertainment retailer.

It's only recently that you can actually use your iPad without first installing iTunes on your computer, but with the release of iOS 5 you can activate your device and get all the latest system updates without the need to manually connect it to your computer. However, there is a lot more to iTunes than allowing iPad functionality, not least the ability to convert your CD collection to MP3 format and copy the tracks to your device, browse for all the latest entertainment and apps at the iTunes and App Stores and enjoy the many new features that iCloud provides. Here we show you the basics.

"It's only recently that you can actually use your iPad without installing iTunes"

iTunes Getting to know the software

01 The Library

Your media is broken down by type, like music, films, television shows, podcasts, books and apps for your iOS devices, all of which you can acquire from the iTunes Store. The last one on the list, Radio, lets you listen to online radio stations for free.

02 The Store

To access Apple's online media store, move your cursor to the Store section in the Sidebar and click on iTunes Store. The front page is geared towards entertainment, showing you the latest and most popular songs and albums, films and TV shows (books can only be purchased from your iOS device).

Browsing the App Store

Helping you find the apps you need in seconds

Categories
Narrow down your search by browsing through a specific category. To access this menu, click on the small triangle to the right of 'App Store'

Search and find
If none of these are of any help, you can always use the good old-fashioned search field. Start typing and a list of options will appear for you to choose from

How do I choose what to add to my iPad?
By default, iTunes is designed to take care of that for you: even if you have more media than can fit in your iPad, it'll choose which ones to add, and which to leave behind. But if you'd like more control over the process, start by clicking on the iPad in the Devices section. From there, you'll have options in the various tabs to select which songs, films or apps you'd like to include. There are multiple ways of doing this, which will be explained in other parts of this book.

New & Noteworthy
Sometimes a recommendation is all you need, and the New & Noteworthy section shows you a selection of staff favourites that you may feel suit your exact needs

Top Charts
Looking at the bestselling apps can help you decide what to get. This one on the front page shows the top sellers irrespective of their category (categories also have their own charts)

03 Finding the apps

To get to the App Store and start browsing for programs for your iPad, check out the menu bar, top of the main part of the iTunes interface, and click on App Store. Once there, you'll find two buttons at the top, one labelled iPhone, the other iPad. Click on iPad.

04 Connecting your iPad

After activating your iPad, it'll appear in the Sidebar under the Devices section. Click on its name and you'll gain access to your device. You can use that section to select which media to add and which apps to install, or just let iTunes add everything automatically.

Sync your music collection

Here's how easy it is to sync your music collection from a computer to the iPad

It might not exactly be pocketable, but the iPad is easily Apple's best music player to date. Its 9.7-inch display makes it easy to browse the music library, album artwork looks gorgeous when viewed full-screen and the Library found in the desktop version makes a comeback, giving quick access to podcasts, audiobooks, genius mixes and more. We can say with confidence that the iPad is the most fun way to listen to music.

Getting music onto your iPad is a simple process through iTunes. It's possible to sync tracks, albums or your entire music library. iTunes remembers your settings, so whenever your iPad is plugged into the computer it automatically syncs any new music tracks to the device. By spending just a few minutes setting up your music sync options, you'll never have to manually transfer tracks and albums again.

iTunes Get your music on your iPad

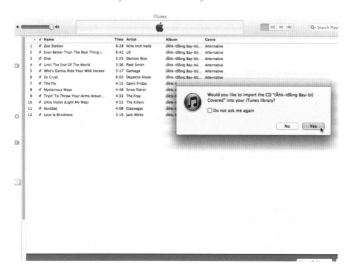

01 Import tunes

First, ensure you have music tracks in your iTunes Library. Insert a CD into the drive and you will be asked if you want to import it. Click 'Yes'.

02 Get to your music

Connect your iPad to your computer and then you can either drag songs manually from your library to your device or click on the 'Music' tab.

03 Choose what to sync

From here you can choose what to sync. Once you're happy with the selection, click the Apply/Sync button at the bottom of the screen.

04 Get playing

Once the syncing process has been completed, turn on your iPad and open the Music app located in the dock at the bottom of the screen.

Sync movies onto your iPad

We explain how easy it is to copy movies from your desktop computer to an iPad

Movies look amazing on the iPad screen. Whether laying in bed or sitting on a train with the iPad in your hands, the display shows off movies with vivid clarity. It gets even better if the movie has been purchased or rented through the iTunes Store, as the iPad will display detailed information about the film and enable users to skip directly to a particular chapter with just one tap of the finger. For those with an Apple TV it's also possible to wirelessly stream any movie to the device from your iPad, enabling you to watch films on a high-definition TV and control the playback using the iPad's touch screen display, but more on that later.

In this tutorial we'll explain how easy it is to sync movies from your desktop computer to the iPad using iTunes. In next to no time you'll be up and running with a selection of great movies on your iPad.

iTunes Sync your movies to your iPad

01 Get ready
Ensure you have movies to sync in iTunes. Films can be purchased from the iTunes Store, or copied to your iTunes Library in MOV or MP4 format.

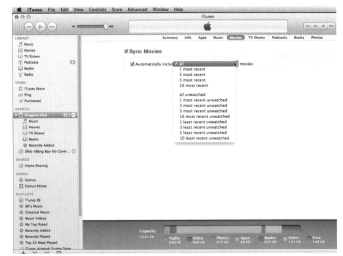

02 Select films
Connect your iPad and click on it in iTunes, then select the Films tab at the top of the screen. If unselected, check the top Sync Films button.

03 Sync!
Select the films that you wish to sync, but keep aware of the file sizes. Once you're happy, click the Apply/Sync button at the bottom of the screen.

04 Get watching
Once the films have copied you can watch them from the Videos app. If purchased from the Store, they will include chapters for easy navigation.

Copy TV shows to your iPad

The iPad's perfect for watching programmes on the go. Here's how to sync TV shows from a Mac/PC

With its relatively large 9.7-inch display and lengthy battery life, the iPad is pretty much the perfect portable television. Its screen is large enough to be easily viewed by more than one person and all images look fantastic on its colourful, high-resolution screen. For anyone who travels around a lot, it's the perfect way to keep entertained on long journeys, and because the iPad is so portable you can continue watching wherever you are in your home.

Getting TV shows onto your iPad is a simple process. By opening the iTunes app you can purchase the latest episodes of your favourite show and download them directly to the device. Alternatively it's possible to sync all the shows on your desktop computer to the iPad by using the desktop version of iTunes. Follow us through this tutorial as we explain how easy it is to sync your TV shows in just four steps. You'll have all of your favourite TV programmes ready to watch on your iPad in no time.

iTunes Watch downloaded television shows on your iPad

01 Go shopping

Go to the iTunes Store and then click on the 'TV Programmes' tab at the top. Here you can browse, purchase and download shows to your computer.

02 Plug and sync

Plug your iPad into the computer. Once it has synced, select it from the grey bar on the left. Next, click on TV Programmes at the top of the screen.

03 Select shows

If Sync TV Programmes isn't already checked, tick it to enable syncing. Once you're happy with the selection of TV shows, click the Apply/Sync button.

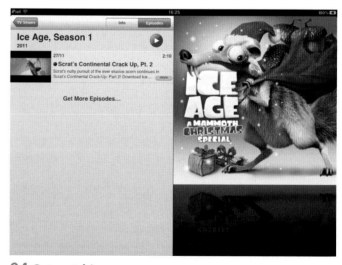

04 Get watching

You can view TV shows from the Videos app on your iPad. Simply open the app and you'll see a TV Shows button at the top of the screen.

Sync podcasts onto your iPad

Discover how to sync podcasts from your desktop computer to an iPad

 Think of podcasts as individual radio shows without the music – some are a few minutes long, others hours in length, and they can be listened to from within the Music app on your iPad. Once you've found a great podcast it's possible to subscribe to it from the iPad's iTunes app, enabling your desktop computer or iPad to automatically download the latest episodes as soon as they're available, ready for you to enjoy. With podcasts you can pick and choose the subjects that interest you, enabling you to skip the

annoying adverts and subject matters that you normally sit through when listening to the radio.

In this tutorial we'll explain how to subscribe to podcasts and sync them between your desktop computer and iPad. It's a simple process done entirely through iTunes. Once you've subscribed to a handful of podcasts you'll find yourself with hours of free entertainment, and wondering how you ever lived without them.

iTunes Listen to podcasts on your iPad

01 Download new podcasts

Open iTunes on your Mac or PC, click on the iTunes Store button then choose Podcasts from the menu at the top of the screen.

02 Plug and sync

Once you've got the podcasts, plug your iPad into your Mac/PC. Click your iPad from the grey side panel, then the Podcasts button at the top.

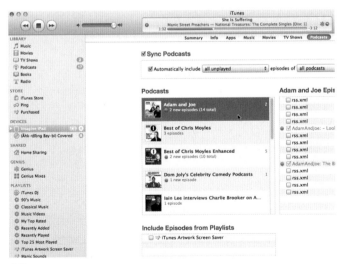

03 Syncing options

From the Podcasts window you can choose to sync individual podcasts, entire subscriptions or only the podcasts with new episodes available.

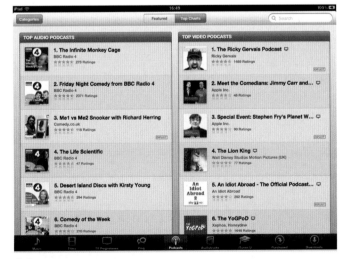

04 Podcasts on your iPad

You can play synced podcasts from the Music app. To get podcasts without a Mac/PC, open the iTunes app and you'll find a Podcasts button.

Setting up

Learn how to sync books

Find out how to sync books with your iPad, and where to download the latest titles

Before the iPad was even announced, media pundits were declaring it to be the saviour of print media. Now that it's been in the hands of customers for a year, it's beginning to justify that claim, as the iPad is a fantastic device for reading books and magazines for a number of reasons. Its large 9.7-inch display makes reading text a joy, the vivid colour screen makes images look even better than their printed counterparts, its support for multimedia means videos and web links can be embedded in books, it's

possible to change the font and text size, look up words with a dictionary and easily control the brightness for when reading in a low-lit environment. The list goes on.

eBooks can either be synced from a desktop computer or purchased directly from Apple's iBooks app – and if downloading books to your computer, you can also use the 'Automatic Downloads' iCloud feature (go to Settings> Store and activate the options). Here we show you how to sync from iTunes.

iTunes Sync eBooks to your iPad

01 Go shopping
Go to the iTunes Store and click on the 'Books' tab at the top of the screen. Books you purchase and download will be added to 'Books' in your library.

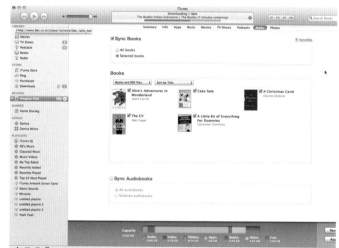

02 Books window
Turn on your iPad and plug it into the computer. After syncing, click on your iPad from the grey side bar, then the Books option at the top of the screen.

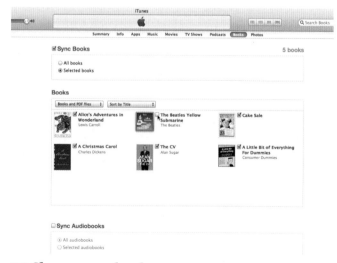

03 Choose your books
You can sync every book by checking the All Books button, or alternatively select your books of choice. Click the Sync/Apply button once you're ready.

04 Download in iBooks
If you install the free iBooks app on your iPad then you can also download books from within by tapping the 'Store' button in the top-right corner.

Sync photos on your iPad

Discover how easy it is to sync photographs from your Mac/PC to an iPad

The iPad is the perfect device for displaying photos. Thanks to its Multi-Touch support it's easy to swipe through images, zoom into areas and create slide-shows. It's by far the best way to show off your latest holiday snaps as the device can be passed from person to person, and because the Photos app is so intuitive it can be used by anyone – even children.

There are a handful of ways to get your favourite photos onto your iPad. They can be synced from a Mac/PC, emailed or imported from an SD card and, thanks to the wonder of iCloud's Photo Stream feature, even beamed wirelessly to your device automatically. In this tutorial we'll explain how easy it is to transfer batches of images from your computer using iTunes.

iTunes Get your photos on your iPad via iTunes

01 Plug in

Open iTunes on your Mac/PC, then plug the iPad into the computer and they'll sync. Once done, click on your iPad from the grey side bar on the left.

02 iPad summary

You'll see a summary of your iPad. At the top of the screen are various buttons for syncing media – click on the Photos button at the far end.

03 Choose your photos

Here you'll see an option to sync photos from your Mac or PC. Click on the check box and choose a folder from your computer. When correct, click OK.

04 Activate Photo Stream

To get all photos automatically pushed to your iPad from your computer or iPhone, go to Settings> Photos and turn Photo Stream on.

App used: Settings

Time needed: 5 minutes

How to use iPad Settings

The Settings app is the epicentre of your iPad. Here you can customise everything from how apps work to the look and feel of the display

 On the first page of the iPad screen is an app called Settings. This controls how your iPad works, allows individual apps to be configured and sets the look and feel of the screens. With it, you can enforce security, log on to Wi-Fi networks, save battery power, add signatures to emails, configure the web browser Safari to use specific search engines and much, much more. It is, perhaps, the most important app on your iPad. Learn what it has to offer and how you can change or configure things and you will take control of the iPad to make it work the way you want it to.

In this tutorial we are going to introduce you to some of the key features within Settings – the ones that you may want to check out straight away to get yourself acquainted to the system. More specific tutorials will follow to show you functions in more depth, but for now, let's delve into the nerve centre of this incredible piece of kit.

> "Learn what the Settings have to offer and make the iPad work the way you want it to"

Settings Work your way around the iPad's control system

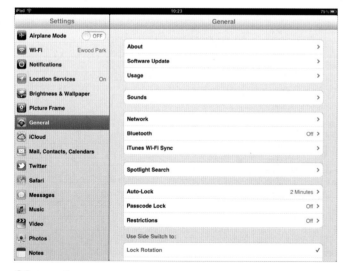

01 Into the Settings
Turn your iPad on and slide the bar across to unlock it. On the very first screen is the Settings app. Tap once on it to launch. There are a great number of parameters but you'll find a lot of useful things to tweak in the 'General' section. If this isn't automatically selected, tap on it now.

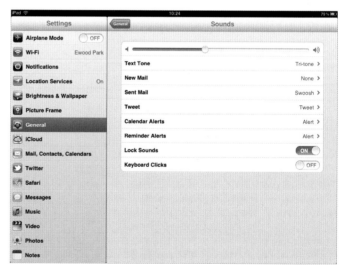

02 Changing the sounds
One of the first things to check out is the sound settings; tap on Sounds and customise these options by sliding the setting to On or Off and sliding your finger along the volume to change it. The General section also lets you control Bluetooth, Date & Time settings and much more so explore here.

The Settings menu laid out in full

Work your way around this user-friendly settings menu

Wireless updates
With iOS 5 you no longer need to connect your iPad to a computer in order to update the system software. Just choose 'Software Update' do get the latest iOS (if available) beamed directly to your device

Master the options
The Settings app controls lots of different features of the iPad and they are all available simply by tapping on the entry for each one and then making the changes required. Some of the most useful include using a graphic equaliser with your music, different fonts with Notes and selecting from Google, Yahoo! Or Bing as your search engine in Safari. To set the music preference, tap on the iPod entry and then on EQ and you can select from a range of music styles and also boost or reduce the base and optimise for speech.

Location, Location
Tap on this section to turn on or off the location services. This allows the iPad to find your co-ordinates using GPS, Wi-Fi and cellular data for things like the Map app

Lock settings
Use Auto-Lock to decide how long you want the iPad to wait for inactivity before it locks, and use Passcode Lock if you want to set a password for when you turn on your iPad

Multitasking Gestures
Here you can turn on or off multitasking gestures, which allow you to use certain swipes of your fingers, such as swipe up, left, right or pinch with four or five fingers, to control your iPad

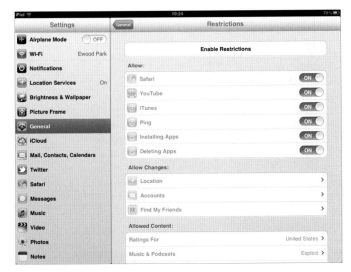

03 Enable Restrictions
The General section also has one of the most important settings options, especially if you let your kids play with the iPad. Here you can turn off in-app purchases, access to iTunes and much more. Just tap Enable Restrictions and you are prompted to set a passcode. Make it memorable.

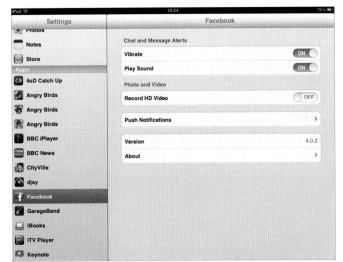

04 App Settings
The Settings menu also lets you change the options for any apps you have downloaded. Just tap on the app you want to change the settings on and you have access to the options. As usual, move sliders to On or Off depending on your preferences to that function.

App used:
Mail

Time needed:
5 minutes

Access email on your iPad

While email works perfectly well on the iPhone it really comes into its own on the iPad's larger screen. This handy tutorial will let you set up your own personal account

 In today's digital age using email is one of the most essential ways of being able to stay in touch with friends and family, as well as being a pretty vital tool in the business world. While both the iPhone and iPod touch are perfectly capable of displaying email, the iPad is just so much better due to its larger size, making it a much superior option. The virtual keyboard makes it far easier and quicker to type on (especially when you need to write longer mails) making it far more practical to use.

This step-by-step tutorial will not only show you how to set up a new or existing email account for use on the iPad and beyond, but will also take you through the fundamentals of reading and sending email. Once set up you'll be able to use existing accounts at will, quickly reply and forward mail that you receive, and, most importantly, ensure that you stay in touch with friends and loved ones. Basically you will never look at your iPad in the same way again.

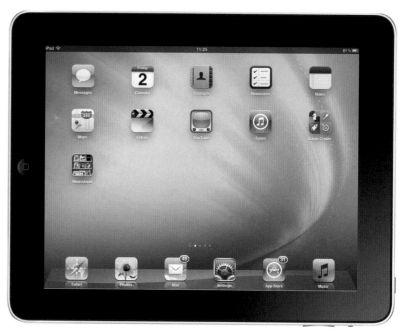

"You will never look at your iPad in the same way again"

Settings Set up an email account on your iPad

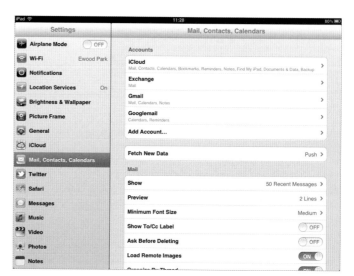

01 Set things up

In order to set up an email account you will need to first enter the Settings of your iPad. Look at the icons on the first page of your iPad until you find one with a large cog and two smaller cogs. Tap on it to continue to the Settings menu.

02 Find your mail

Upon entering Settings you'll find a row of different icons down the left-hand side of the screen. Look for and select 'Mail, Contacts, Calendars' in order to continue. Now look on the right-hand side of the screen and tap on Add Account…

Viewing mail

Look for the mail tab on the left-hand side of the page in Mail. Tap on it and you will instantly be shown your latest mail. Scroll down for more emails

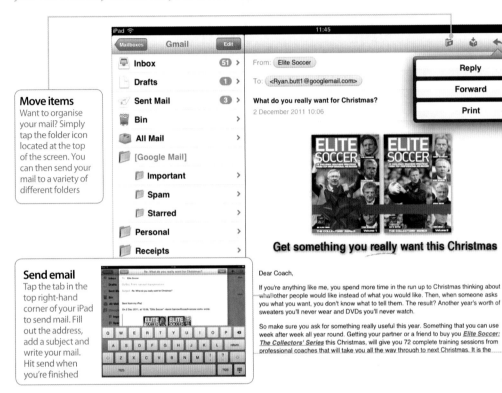

Forwarding Mail
If you need to reply to an email hit the arrow icon near the top of the screen. You can then reply to the sender or forward the message on

Move items
Want to organise your mail? Simply tap the folder icon located at the top of the screen. You can then send your mail to a variety of different folders

Send email
Tap the tab in the top right-hand corner of your iPad to send mail. Fill out the address, add a subject and write your mail. Hit send when you're finished

Adding more accounts
If you have the need for additional accounts (perhaps a work account or the account of your significant other) it's relatively easy to add them. All you need to do is re-follow the previous steps for setting up an account. Once you've done that when you enter your mail you will see an 'Accounts' tab in the top left-hand side of the screen. Simply tap on this tab to be taken to all the other accounts set up on your iPad. Select the one you want and you can instantly access your other mail. Very handy.

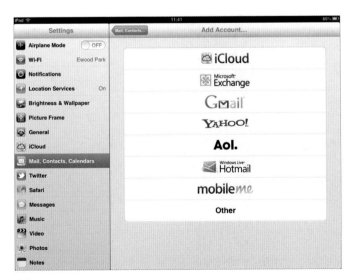

03 Make your choice

You'll now be presented with six different account options. They are Microsoft Exchange, MobileMe, Google Mail, Yahoo! Mail, AOL and Other (which will allow you access accounts like Hotmail). Whether you want to create a new account or add an existing one the process is as follows…

04 You've got mail!

After choosing your account you'll be presented with the following screen. All you need to do here is fill in the relevant information for each section. Once this is done simply tap on Save in the top right-hand corner. Congratulations, you have mail.

Setting up

Change Wallpaper on your iPad

We show you how to quickly customise the background of your home and lock screens

 With the iPad, Apple has allowed users the ability to change the background of the home screen as well as the lock screen. This may seem like a trivial addition to the software set but for Apple it's pretty big. It is a company that deals in absolutes and who employs a closed system to prevent people making the environment look bad. So we're glad that we get to add a little individuality to the home screen and we're also pretty pleased when we discovered you can also have two different images for the lock screen and home screen.

Making changes to the system is very simple; it works in a very similar way to the iPhone, only you can see much more of the action path that you take to get to a change in settings. This makes the system clearer, more memorable and much easier to use. Proficiency at this simple task should give you the courage to explore the settings further to get even more use from your iPad and make improvements to the way it works for you. Whether it's an image from the iPad's supplied Wallpaper set or a photo from your album, following this step-by-step tutorial will instantly customise your iPad and have it looking the way you want it to.

Settings Change wallpaper

01 Cog tapper
Load the Settings by tapping the Settings button in the iPad home screen. You will be taken to this screen. Tap on Brightness & Wallpaper on the left-hand side.

02 Wallpaper
Here you can adjust the brightness if you deem it necessary. Simply tap on the pictures beneath the word 'Wallpaper' in the right-hand column of the screen.

03 Options
You now have several options from which to get a picture from. Choose the album that you wish to pick from. Tap on that album to then bring up the contents.

Customising your home screen

Making the most of all that screen real estate

Simplicity
As always Apple makes interfaces easy to use. There's no mass of dialogue and the system breeds confidence to try more complex tasks and procedures

Finger fun
While positioning your picture you'll be able to see just how responsive the iPad touch screen is. It's a testament to hardware and software unity

Kill it
Apple also makes it easy for you to change your mind and go back to the last action. In this case just hit the Cancel button

Great resolution
The iPad screen has a fantastic 1024 x 768-pixel resolution at 132 pixels per inch (ppi) resolution for viewing images so having a cool pic behind your icons is a must

Settings
The settings system on the iPad follows the same pathways as those on the iPhone, only instead of shunting the view to the left or right as options are chosen, you can see the result of your choice to the right of the static options list.

04 Preview

Once in the album of your choice, make your final selection and then simply tap on that picture. A zooming animation will automatically take you to a preview screen.

05 Top options

Use a pinch, reverse pinch and swipe to position the image and then pick from the options at the top of the screen: you can pick Set Lock Screen, Set Home Screen or Set Both.

06 Check it

Once you've tapped an option you'll be taken back to the home screen where you can see your changes. Use the sleep button if you wish to view the lock screen.

Setting up

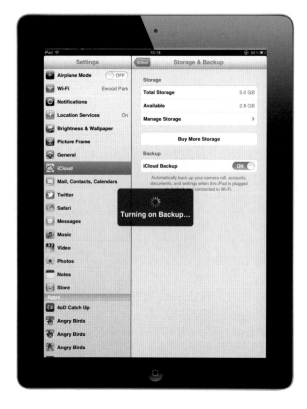

Use iCloud to back up your iPad

With iCloud, you can back up all of your important iPad data to your own virtual hard drive

Your iPad is like a bank vault where all kinds of important stuff is stored. So what happens if your iPad gets lost or goes awry? Nothing, that's what. Thanks to iCloud, all of your data is automatically backed up and kept safely in your own cloud storage space. When your iPad is connected to a power source and a Wi-Fi network, all of your media, photos, videos, settings, app data and messages are backed up.

When you set up a new iOS device or need to restore the information on the one you already have, iCloud Backup does all the heavy lifting. All you have to do is ensure that your device is connected to Wi-Fi, enter your Apple ID and all of your important data will appear on your device without you having to worry about a thing. As you will have read elsewhere in this book, the benefits of using iCloud are vast, and the way in which it goes about its business in the background without you having to worry is just another prime example of how Apple is striving to make your life easier.

"Another prime example of how Apple is striving to make your life easier"

iCloud Activate iCloud and backup your data

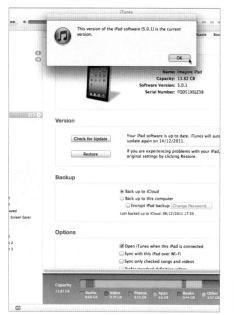

01 Update to iOS 5
iCloud is a service that comes as part of iOS 5, so connect your device to your computer through iTunes and check to ensure you have the latest free software update installed on your device.

02 Launch Settings
From your iPad's Home screen, launch your Settings app, and in the left-hand column will be a new category called 'iCloud'. Tap on this and then enter your Apple ID and password.

03 Set up
Once your personal iCloud has been set up and you have selected which apps you would like to sync, tap on the 'Storage & Backup' option at the bottom of the list.

Backing up with iCloud

Once activated, your iCloud will back up your stuff automatically

Manage your space
You can see how your free 5GB allocation of cloud storage space is used by tapping on the 'Manage Storage' option

Instant backup
You can back up your data by tapping the 'Backup Now' option. Do this if you change your settings or buy new media

Backup
When the 'iCloud Backup' option is turned on, all settings, documents, media and photos will be automatically backed up when your device is connected to a power supply and Wi-Fi

Progress bar
When your device is backing up, a progress bar will appear that shows how far along the process it is. You can cancel the backup at any time

Manage your storage
By tapping on the 'Storage & Backup' option in the iCloud Settings screen and then going to 'Manage Storage', you'll be able to see exactly how your iCloud is used with individual breakdowns of how much of your free 5GB of space your apps use. If you find that you need to purchase more space then you can do so through this screen.

04 Turn on Backup
On this screen you will be able to monitor and manage your iCloud storage space, but more importantly you will see an option called 'iCloud Backup'. Ensure that the slider is moved to 'On'.

05 Wait for the activation
You'll be presented with a message saying that your iPad will no longer sync to iTunes when connected to your computer, so tap 'OK' and wait for a minute while the Backup feature is activated.

06 Start backing up
Your iPad will now back up when connected to a power source and a Wi-Fi network, but you can perform the backup whenever you want by accessing this screen and tapping 'Backup Now'.

Getting started

All the basics are covered right here to get you in control of your iPad

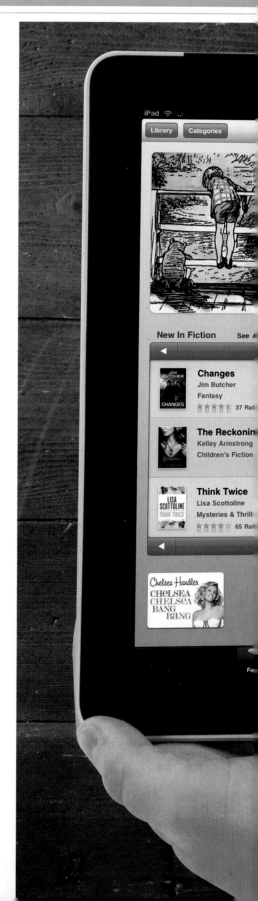

"Personalise your Notification Center and tailor all aspects of how your device gets messages to you"

52
Move icons and create folders

68
Add a calendar event

86
Find your way with Maps

92
Explore iTunes

App used:
N/A

Time needed:
3 minutes

Moving icons and using folders

Once you've installed lots of apps, the screens start to fill up and it gets harder to find things. Discover how to organise your apps and keep your iPad tidy

Whenever a new app is installed, it just gets added to the end of the existing list, or if there's a gap anywhere, it can appear there. This is fine when you only have a handful of apps, but after a couple of months with your iPad, the screens start to fill up and it all looks disorganised and messy. Fortunately it can all be organised into areas of similar functions, such as games on one page, utilities on another and reference apps on a page as well. You can reorganise your iPad screens using iTunes, where it is easy to create extra screens, even if the current ones are full, but it's also possible to move icons around directly on the iPad. Also, you can create as many folders as you like and bundle apps together to make your display very neat and tidy. The final benefits are that unwanted apps can be deleted and must-have apps can be added to the favourites bar at the bottom of every screen.

"You can bundle apps together to make your display very neat and tidy"

iPad Home   Keep your iPad organised

01 Activate the wiggle

Turn your iPad on so that you are looking at your Home screen. If you have lots of apps then the icons for them will be spread over subsequent screens. To arrange them together tap and hold an app you want to move until all the apps start to wiggle.

02 Move the app

Still holding down on the app, drag your finger to the edge of the screen you want to move to. The apps will then scroll sideways to give you the next screen. Move your finger over the place you want the app to go and then let go of it.

Inside the new folder display

Edit the folder name and move apps inside it

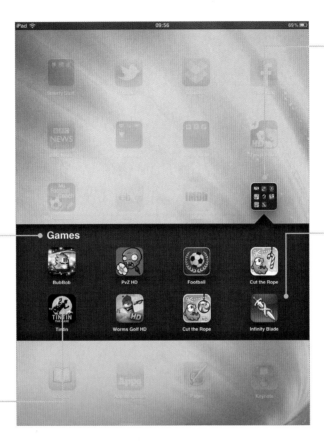

Edit the folder name
Tap a folder to open it. Tap and hold an app inside to go into wiggle editing mode. You can now remove or change the folder name

Take an app out
While in wiggle mode you can drag an app out of the folder again simply by tapping and holding and then moving outside the folder area

Rearrange apps inside the folder
If there's lots of apps inside a folder, rearrange them by tapping and holding and then dragging to a new position. The other apps will shuffle along and move

Delete an app in a folder
To remove an app that is inside a folder simply tap on the 'X' icon on the top-left corner. You will still have a backup inside iTunes

Favourite and unwanted apps
When in wiggle mode a little cross appears on the top-left corner of all the apps. Tap on this to delete the app directly from your iPad. You can't delete the ones the iPad comes with. The favourites bar at the bottom of the screen comes with six slots for your favourite apps. Again, in wiggle mode you can move them around, drag them on or off the bar or simply add your new, favourite app to the ones there by dragging and releasing the app over it.

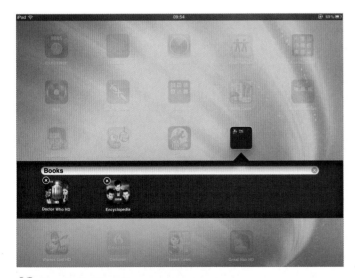

03 Create folders for common apps

Press the Home button to return your iPad to normal. To create folders though, drop an app over the top of one you want it to appear in a folder with. A folder is then instantly created with a name that reflects the type of apps if they are fairly similar.

04 Rename the folder

If the folder name isn't to your liking, simply tap on the 'X' icon to delete it and tap in the text field to enter your own. When complete, press the Home button twice to exit. To add more apps to the same folder, simply drag and drop them into it.

App used:
Safari

Time needed:
5 minutes

Use tabbed browsing in Safari

Discover how the already pleasurable experience of Safari has been improved by some great iOS 5 enhancements

Surfing the web on your Apple device has always been a simple and pleasurable experience, but iOS 5 adds some welcome tweaks to ensure that the experience is made even easier. One of the most prominent enhancements is the use of tabs to manage your open Safari webpages.

When opening new pages in iOS 4, you were briefly taken out of the main window to be presented with your pages laid out on a grid, which you tapped to call up individual pages. iOS 5 arranges all open pages in tabs at the top of the main window, allowing you to access them from the same interface. Two other new features that have been subtly worked into Safari are Reading List and Reader. With Reading List, you can save articles to read offline, and upload them to your iCloud. Reader supplies a similarly handy service by allowing you to read articles free from on-screen clutter, such as images and adverts, so that you can be unhampered by visual distractions. Read on to explore tabbed browsing.

"iOS 5 brings tweaks to Safari to ensure the experience is made even easier"

Safari Open multiple pages using tabs

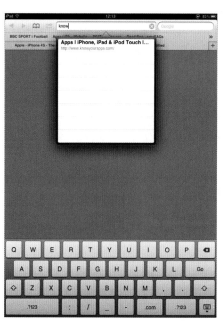

01 Launch Safari

Visit any webpage in Safari. If you have bookmarks stored then these will be laid out across the top of the window. Tap one to go to that particular page.

02 Open new tab

Simply tap the '+' icon in the top right-hand corner of Safari's interface, and a new page will become available in a separate tab near the top of the screen.

03 Adding tabs

Keep adding tabs by pressing the '+' icon to call up a new window. As more tabs are added, the existing ones will be pushed further along the top.

Your new-look Safari window

Little enhancements that make a big difference

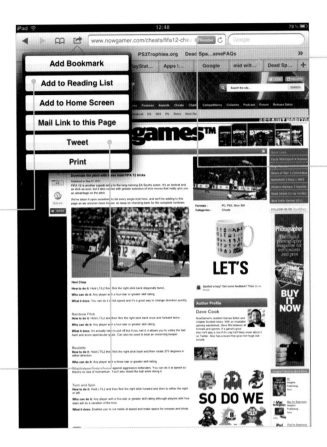

Add Bookmark
Add to Reading List
Add to Home Screen
Mail Link to this Page
Tweet
Print

Your tabs
All of the webpages that you currently have open will be displayed as tabs at the top of the screen. Tap on a tab to access it instantly

Reading List
Another new Safari enhancement is Reading List. If you're running short on time, add an article to your list, and you'll be able to finish it later – even on a different device

Safari Reader
To read certain articles without clutter, such as pictures or ads, tap the Reader icon in the address bar, and all non-article material will be stripped away

Tweet from within
With Twitter integrated in iOS 5, you can tweet from within your favourite apps without having to copy links into a separate Twitter app

Cloud connect
Safari works with your own personal iCloud, meaning that any articles you add to your Reading List are synced to your iCloud and stored, so you can start reading them on an iPad, and pick them up where you left off on your iPhone later.

04 Accessing tabs
Using tabbed browsing is quicker and more efficient than the format favoured by the previous iOS, as you can access any tabbed page by tapping on the tab.

05 Closing tabs
Upon reaching your limit, you will no longer be able to add new tabs without deleting existing ones. To do this, simply just open a tab and then tap on 'X'.

06 Organising your tabs
If wish to rearrange the tabs at the top of your browser window, then simply press and hold on a particular tab, and drag it left or right to reposition it among the other tabs.

App used:
Safari

 Time needed:
10 minutes

Get more from bookmarks on the iPad

The iPad has many uses, but one of its main strengths is browsing the web.
Like the Mac the iPad uses Safari – here's how to get the most out of it

The iPad is great for many things and the extra applications available for it expand its usability even further. Some of the built-in applications will get more use than anything you download from the App Store, however. One of the apps you're likely to use more often than any other is Safari.

Browsing the web on your iPad was already a fun and intuitive experience with Apple's flagship web browser, but since iOS 5 was released the app has enjoyed a few enhancements to make it more on par with its Mac counterparts. These include tabbed web pages (so that you can keep visited sites open in neatly arranged tabs for easy access), Reading List (which keeps track of articles you have been reading but haven't had the chance to finish) and Reader (which allows you to read pages with all of the ads and clutter stripped out). You can also tie your bookmarks to your iCloud account, meaning that they will be synced across all of your devices. Here's how to get started with Safari…

"Tie bookmarks to your iCloud account, syncing them across all of your devices"

Using bookmarks

Working your way around
Safari bookmarks

Bookmarks bar
You can store all your most oft-visited websites here but remember to turn the 'Show bookmarks' option on in Settings. If you edit the names you can store more links here too

Address bar
Of course, you can still just get to your favourite website the old fashioned way by typing them directly into the address bar

Search
The search bar is visible all the time and by default is set to Google, but if you want you can switch from Google to Yahoo! if you prefer

Add bookmark icon
The most useful icons are here. Add a new page, see your bookmarks and when you want to add a bookmark, tap here to start the process off

iCloud
If you have activated your iCloud account then you can sync your bookmarks from your computer or iPhone to your iPad, that way you won't have to add them all manually. To make sure you are syncing your bookmarks go to Settings and iCloud, then ensure that the 'Bookmarks' slider it switched to 'On'. Now let the auto-syncing commence!

Safari Go further with bookmarks

01 Add a website
Navigate to the website you want to add to your home screen. When it has loaded tap on the arrow symbol in the toolbar and tap 'Add to Home Screen'.

02 Give your icon a name
When you tap on 'Add to Home Screen' it will add the title of the page, but you can edit this to something more appropriate. Tap 'Add' when you're done.

03 Get rid of a home screen icon
If you're not using your bookmarked home screen icon very much, it's easy to get rid of it. Simply tap and hold until the 'X' appears at the top right and tap that.

04 Add a bookmark
You'll be familiar with internet bookmarks and you can add them on the iPad too. Just tap the arrow symbol on the toolbar and then simply tap 'Add bookmark'.

05 Name your bookmark
After you've tapped on Add bookmark you'll have to give your new bookmark a name. This will be automatically chosen, but you can easily change it to something more memorable to you.

06 Get to your bookmarks
To see your bookmarks tap on the open book icon in the toolbar. All of your bookmarks will be listed under the History and Bookmarks Bar folders here.

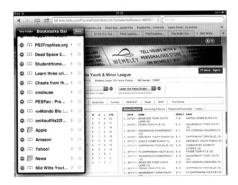

07 Delete a bookmark
To remove a bookmark from your folder tap on the bookmarks icon and then tap on Edit. A red icon with a '–' symbol will appear; tap it and then tap 'Delete'.

08 Move the bookmark
If you'd like to keep the bookmark in the bookmarks bar, tap Edit and then tap on your bookmark. Available folders will appear, so tap the Bookmarks Bar folder.

09 Show the Bookmarks bar
The bookmarks bar may not be showing up for you; it's easy to remedy this. Go to Settings>Safari and make sure that Always Show Bookmarks Bar is set to on.

App used: Safari

Time needed: 5 minutes

De-clutter the web with Safari Reader

Thanks to a new Safari feature, you can read fresh web content devoid of intrusive ads and page furniture

Browsing web pages through Safari on your iPad is a pleasurable experience thanks to its intuitive interface and useful features designed to make surfing the internet as effortless as possible.

The app got even better too, thanks to the iOS 5 update that introduced additional elements such as tabbed pages and Reading List. But perhaps the best new addition to Safari's arsenal of cool features is Reader.

This feature enables you to read and enjoy web articles free from clutter such as intrusive ad banners and links. If you have accessed a page that can benefit from the Safari Reader function then a 'Reader' icon will be visible in the address bar. Tap on it and the page will undergo an instant transformation into a cleaner, easier-to-read format. What's more, you can increase the font size to make it even easier to read and not get distracted by page furniture. It's quick and easy to use Reader, and when you have read the article and want to return the page to its original state you simply tap the 'Reader' icon again.

"This feature enables you to read and enjoy web articles free from clutter"

Safari How to use Reader

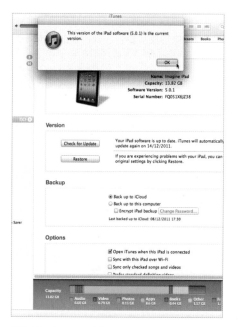

01 Update to iOS 5

Safari Reader is a service that comes as part of iOS 5, so connect your device to your computer through iTunes and ensure that you have the latest free software update installed.

02 Launch Safari

Launch your Safari app and then start browsing. As you access various pages, keep an eye on the address bar for the tell-tale 'Reader' icon that signifies that the page you are on is compatible.

03 Tap 'Reader'

When you find a page that displays the 'Reader' icon, tap on the icon to transform the page into a clear, easy-to-read format. All of the side columns, ads and unnecessary clutter will be removed.

Make pages easier to read

Make web articles cleaner with the tap of a button

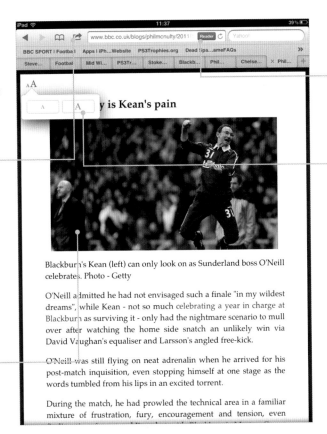

Reader icon
When a page is compatible with Reader, look out for the 'Reader' icon in the address bar and tap it to strip the clutter out of the page

Reading List
To store the article safely, without having to create a new bookmark, tap on the sharing icon and choose 'Add to Reading List'

Change font
By tapping on the font icon you can increase the size of the display font to make the current article even easier to read

A cleaner look
Pages that are being viewed through Reader feature only the main text, with all side panels and ads stripped out for a fresher, uncluttered look

iCloud compatibility
The latest version of Safari that comes with the iOS 5 update is fully compatible with your iCloud, so all of your bookmarks and Reading List articles will be automatically synced, meaning you can continue exactly where you left off on a different iOS 5 device later.

04 Increase font size

To make the page even easier to read, tap on the font icon in the top-left corner of the page. This will enable you to switch between two font sizes, increasing the size of the display font.

05 Add to Reading List

If you don't have time to read all of the current article, then you can add it to your 'Reading List' to read later. Tap on the sharing icon on the top bar and choose 'Add to Reading List'.

06 Return to normal

When you've read the article, tap on the 'Reader' icon again, which will now be displayed in purple, and your page will return to its previous state and you'll be able to continue browsing as normal.

App used:
Safari

Time needed:
10 minutes

Change the default search engine

The built-in search bar in Safari lets you seek out what you need fast, but you don't have to just use Google to provide your answers, Yahoo! and Bing are options too

 When you're searching the web it's second nature to just tap on the toolbar and type out your enquiry. By default Apple has chosen to use Google as the search engine of choice and for many people this will be absolutely fine.

However, Google isn't to everyone's tastes so there's the option to swap to Yahoo! or Bing. As it stands, if you use Safari for your web browsing these are your only choices and you can't even pick your favourite location. For instance, you can't set UK as the location for your preferred results. Some of the third-party web browsers available on the App Store will let you choose from a wider range of default search partners.

Otherwise you can navigate to the homepage of your favourite search engine and set it as an icon on your home screen. This way you'll always start a new browsing session at your desired search engine. However, for the built-in search bar in Safari you're stuck with just three until Apple decides that more are needed.

"If Google isn't to your tastes so you can swap to Yahoo! or Bing"

Safari Swap default search providers on your iPad

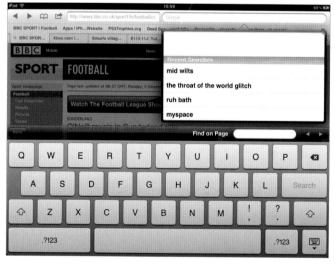

01 Safari search

If you open Safari you'll see the search bar up in the top-right of the screen. In it will be the name of the current default search engine provider, for example in the screenshot above it's Google. When you begin typing the name disappears.

02 Settings

You can't change the search provider within Safari; instead you have to do it from within the Settings app. You need to press the Home button to quit the app and navigate back to your home screen. Find the Settings app and then tap on it.

Search engine selection
Find the perfect search engine for you

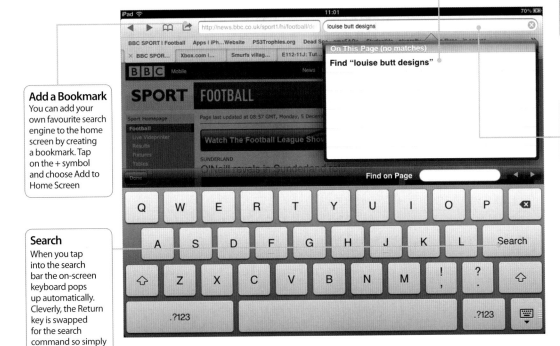

Suggested results
Both Yahoo! and Google offer suggestions based on what you type, that way you don't always have to type the search term fully. Simply tap on the suggestion to immediately see the associated results appear

Add a Bookmark
You can add your own favourite search engine to the home screen by creating a bookmark. Tap on the + symbol and choose Add to Home Screen

Search bar
The search bar in Safari can use either Google, Yahoo! and Bing, you can swap between them but sadly you can't choose another provider if you prefer the competition

Search
When you tap into the search bar the on-screen keyboard pops up automatically. Cleverly, the Return key is swapped for the search command so simply hit that to get the results you want

Third-party browsers
You don't have to use Safari on the iPad as there are a number of alternative browsers available on the App Store. These offer more in the way of functionality too, such as tabbed browsing and a larger range of search provider options. Simply type 'web browser' into the App Store search bar and download a selection; some are free, while others are available for a small fee.

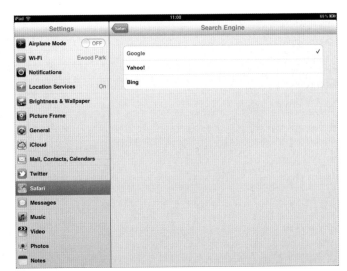

03 Safari settings
In the Settings app you will see the list of options down the left-hand side of the screen. By tapping on Safari you will reveal the options that are available to you. In the main section on the right, tap on Search Engine up at the top, listed under General.

04 Make your selection
The scarcity of options here and size given over to show them off would seem to imply that more search engine options could be accommodated. As it stands, however, you have just the three to choose from. Tap on Google, Yahoo!, or Bing and return to Safari.

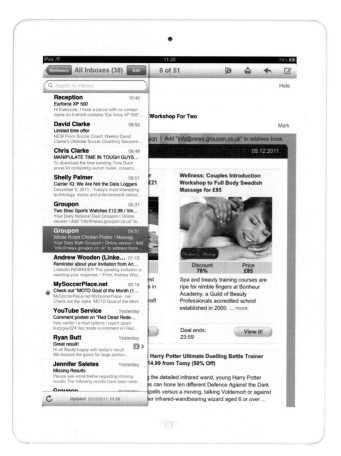

App used:
Mail

Time needed:
15 minutes

Organise your emails quickly

The iPad's Mail app sets a new standard on how emails are managed from touch-enabled tablets

Email is part of everybody's day-to-day life. Most of us start our morning with it. Before, checking for emails would mean starting your fully fledged computer, but with the introduction of the iPhone this habit changed drastically. Most of us were using the device to check emails, but even though the iPhone has a decent Mail application, the small screen and lack of full-size keyboard was a problem. iPad's Mail app, however, takes what is good about it on the iPhone and presents it with large screen and full-size keyboard. This provides the best email experience between the mobile devices.

The Mail app supports most of the current generation technology such as automatic service discovery, Exchange Support, POP/IMAP support and built-in support for MobileMe, Gmail, Yahoo Mail and AOL. The Mail app on the iPad also plays well with other related apps on the iPad, such as the Calendar.

In this tutorial we will look into doing a few of the more important tasks using the Mail app. It's all very easy – let us show you how…

"The iPad takes what is good about Mail on the iPhone and presents it with a full-size keyboard"

Mail Organising emails

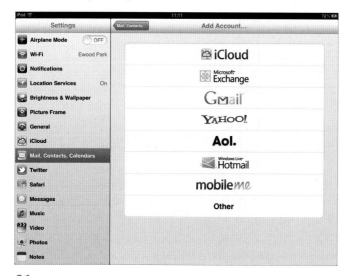

01 Adding an email account

Open Settings and select 'Mail, Contacts, Calendars'. You will now be presented with account types that you can use. Tapping on any one of the supported services will open the pop-up window asking for account details. Fill in the required information to set up your email account.

02 Searching for emails

Search for emails in Mail by typing onto the Search Box and selecting the From, To or Subject fields. Do a full text search by tapping All. By default this will only do a search on the emails that have been downloaded on the iPad. To do a full search you can tap on 'Continue Search on Server…'

You've got mail!

Work your way around the Mail app

Move message
Tap this icon here to move a message to a folder (or mailbox)

Search box
This allows you to search your emails to find a specific one

Refresh mailbox
This checks the mail server for any new messages and downloads them if they are available

Email Protocols
iPad's Mail app supports all major email protocols.

These are:

1. Exchange ActiveSync: Exchange ActiveSync is a data synchronisation protocol that provides push synchronisation of emails, tasks, contacts between ActiveSync enabled devices and servers such as the iPhone.

2. IMAP (Internet Message Access Protocol): IMAP is a protocol for retrieving emails and working with mailboxes on a mail server using an email client. Email clients using IMAP generally leave messages on the server until the user explicitly deletes them. This and other characteristics of IMAP operation allow multiple clients to manage the same mailbox.

3. POP (Post Office Protocol): POP is similar to IMAP but does not provide support for using multiple clients using the same mailbox.

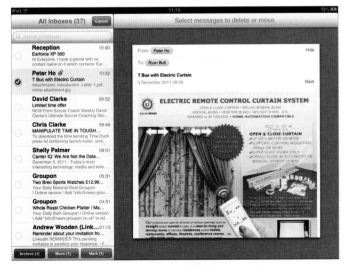

03 Moving messages between folders (mailboxes)

Tap Edit, then select all the messages that you want to move to a different folder, then tap Move. Tapping Move will give you a list of the folders that are available; all you need to do is simply tap on a folder to move the selected messages.

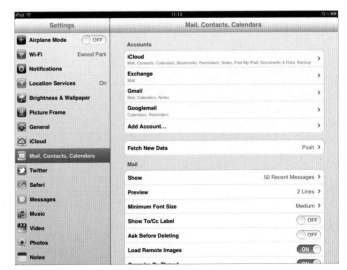

04 Tweak the settings

You can configure a wide range of settings which control how Mail works. To access the settings for Mail, tap Settings (from the home screen), then 'Mail, Contacts, Calendars'. You can change the Account Settings, Mail, Default Account, Signature and more.

App used:
Mail

Time needed:
10 minutes

How to work with attachments

The iPad is better suited for work than an iPhone, and it's especially useful for emailing documents while on the move. We'll show you how the iPad deals with attachments

It's hard to imagine a working day when you don't have to deal with email attachments, and it's likely you're going to be faced with similar tasks while on your iPad. So, how does the iPad handle these? That question will depend on what's attached to your email in the first place.

This step-by-step tutorial will show you how you can work with your iPad to handle common files like photos, iWork or Microsoft Office documents and PDFs. They each behave in slightly different ways but the principle is actually very similar and it will take you next to no time to find your way around the iPad interface. But receiving attachments is only half the story. It's obvious that you'll also need to send them out too, which is why we'll cover that part as well. So pick up your iPad and let's see how all of this works.

"It's hard to imagine a working day when you don't have to deal with email attachments"

Email analysis
The key functions of Mail

Downloading attachments
If you see this downward-pointing arrow on an attachment, it means it hasn't been downloaded to your iPad yet. To get it, tap on it

Send more than one photo attachment
To send multiple photos in the same email message, you need to start from your Photo app's thumbnail section. Tap on the Export button (top right of the interface) and select up to five photos – that's the limit. Although you can copy more and manually paste them to an email, this may fill up the recipient's mailbox, which they might not be too happy about.

The paper clip
Any email containing an attachment will have this little paper clip next to the sender's name. Most of the time, the file will appear as an icon at the bottom of the message

Specialised icons
If the file can be opened in one of your iPad's apps, it'll bear that app's image at the centre of its icon. If the icon is bare it'll only be viewable with Quick Look

Editing attachments
To open a file in another program, tap and hold on the file's icon to reveal this popover menu. A simple tap on the right option will transfer it to that program

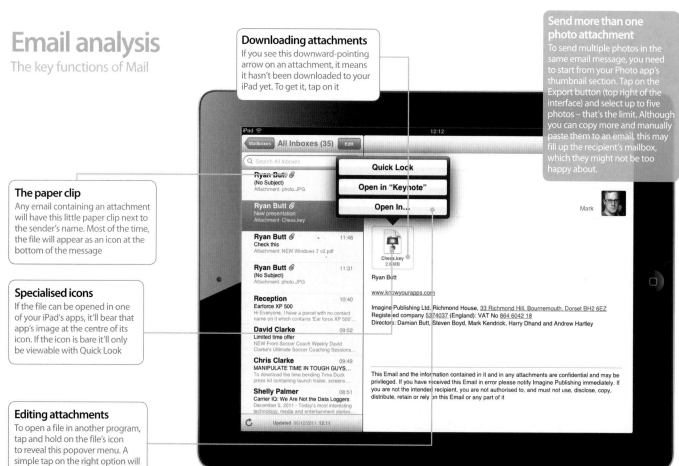

Mail Using attachments

01 Into the Photo app
When you're sent an image via email, adding it to your photo library is really easy: just tap and hold on it to reveal a popover menu, then select 'Save Image'.

02 RTF and PDF files
If you're dealing with RTF files or PDFs, tapping on its icon will open it in Quick Look, where you can view and copy text, but you can't edit anything this way.

03 iWork and Office documents
With other documents, like Keynote or Pages, tapping on it will lead to the Quick Look section, but if you need to edit it, there's another way, which we will show you in step 4.

04 Getting out of Quick Look
To get out of Quick Look tap on the screen. You can choose 'Done' to get back to Mail or 'Open in…' if you own the relevant application. Do the former to leave quick look.

05 Open in an editing app
To get straight to the relevant app without having to go into Quick Look first, tap and hold on the file's icon. This reveals a popover menu. Select 'Open in…'.

06 Copying a photo
Going back to a photo attachment, if you want to use it in iWork but not add it to your library, tap and hold on it, and select Copy from the popover menu that appears.

07 Pasting elsewhere
To open a document in Pages for instance (either an existing one or from an attachment), tap and hold to reveal a menu and select Paste to add that photo.

08 Attaching a file
To attach a file from one of your iWork apps, select a document from the Gallery, tap on the first button in the toolbar (lower left) and choose Send via Mail.

09 Attaching a photo
To send a photo, select it from your Photos app and tap on the export icon (it's found at the top-right of the interface in the middle). Now simply click on Email Photo.

App used: Calendar

 Time needed: 5 minutes

Set the default calendar

The iPad can handle multiple calendars but you may use one more than another. Here's how to set the default

Tuesday 9 One of the main advantages of the iPad is its ability to manage multiple calendars in one very simple interface. You can mix and match your home and work commitments and keep them all in the same place. The colour-coded calendars mean you can know instantly whether the next date in your diary is home, work, or anything else related.

When you're making entries to Calendar on your iPad it selects a default calendar to store the event in. This is great if the default calendar matches the one you use most. However, if you're using it for mainly work-related stuff and the default calendar is for home, you'll have to change it each time you add an event. You can edit the entries to match the calendar after, but this is a time-consuming process.

Changing the default calendar will make entering new appointments a bit faster and cut down on mislabelled entries too. Of course, the time saved is minimal, but it's one less thing to worry about and will help to keep you more organised in the long run.

"It's one less thing to worry about and will help to keep you more organised"

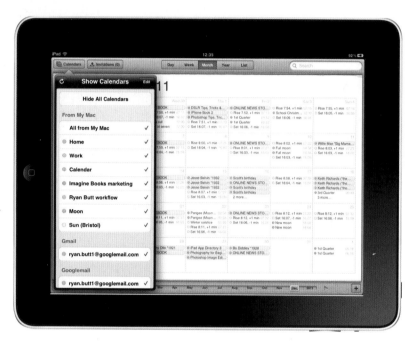

Calendar Change the default calendar

01 Go to Settings

A few of the iPad's application settings are editable from within the app itself, but in this case you need to go to the separate Settings app. Press the Home button and then swipe to the home screen with the Settings app on it. Simply tap to open it.

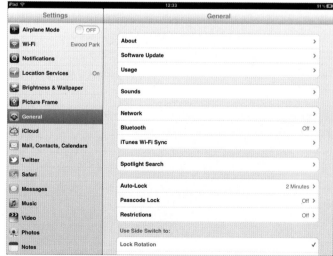

02 Mail, Contacts, Calendars

Over on the right-hand side of the Settings screen you will see all the options available to you and in most cases the General page will be showing. Tap on Mail, Contacts, Calendars just below General to get to the Default Calendar, in the Calendars section (scroll down to see it).

Defining the default calendar
Keeping you in the right place at the right time

Calendars
If you have a number of calendars, you can choose which ones to display by tapping on Calendars at the top-left of the screen. When the list appears simply tap on the tick to hide those entries

Add event
Add a new event by tapping on the + symbol in the bottom right-hand corner of Calendar on your iPad. To edit the settings simply tap on each heading

Default calendar
Each new entry will be put in the default calendar. You can change the default by following the steps here or for one-offs simply tap on Calendar

Repeat event
If you want to set a regular reminder, for someone's birthday or perhaps a regular but finite set of meetings, then tap on repeat and select the appropriate frequency. You will notice that there's a new option in the Add Event pop-up called End Repeat. Tap here and you can choose the exact date you want the repeat to finish or leave it to repeat forever.

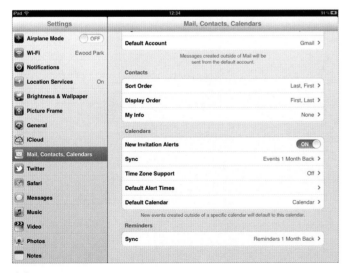

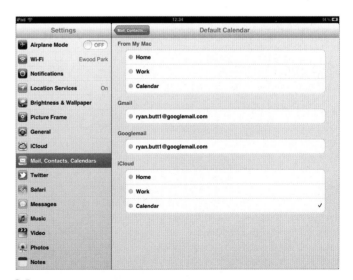

03 Default Calendar
You will need to scroll down by swiping to get to the Default Calendar setting as it is right at the bottom of the page. In the Calendars section the current default calendar will be showing; you can tap on it to access further options that are available.

04 Select your calendar
Here you have a list of all the calendars that are available to you and the currently selected default has a tick next to it. Simply tap on the calendar that you would like to select as the new default. Press the Home key when you're done.

App used:
Calendar

Time needed:
10 minutes

Add an Event in Calendar

If you find yourself struggling to remember what your schedule for the day, week, month or year look like, make sure you never miss an important event with your iPad

Tuesday 9 The Calendar app on the iPhone is pretty useful and very easy to use, but it gets dwarfed by the sheer scale of the iPad equivalent. Like the Contacts app, Apple has gone with the classic analogue look and made the app look like an old-school, physical calendar. Of course, this digital version has a multitude of advantages over a real one. Firstly, you get the beauty of typeface rather than scrawled handwriting. Secondly, it's easy to undo mistakes. Thirdly, you can view it in a number of different ways.

Like all the iPad apps, the Calendar app is easy to use. So easy to use that you'll want to document every move you make using it, from eating breakfast to scheduling business meetings. Adding an event is simplicity itself, and the large screen size means that pop-up windows replace the screen shunting right or left as it does on the iPhone. All you need remains in front of you at all times. Once your events are created they can be edited and you can view them in a number of ways as you change orientation or as you dictate on the top tabs of the app.

"You get the beauty of typeface rather than scrawled handwriting"

Adding an event

You're never more than a few taps away from adding or editing an event to your calendar, and the interface is extremely simple

Top tabs
These tabs change the view of the calendar. They are great if you want specific details for a day or an overview of an entire month. Tapping to change them is as intuitive as computing gets

Search
This is a really useful function that negates the need for flipping through countless pages. You just type in a parameter and the app will find what you are looking for

Pop-ups
The size of the screen means that pop-ups can jump from any event whenever you tap them. A great way to view information

Slide navigation
You can navigate through dates on the bottom of the app by sliding your finger or just tapping on a date

Syncing
If you have an iCloud account you can opt to sync calendars when you set up your Mail account. When the iPad is connected to Wi-Fi or 3G it will use the push system to update any other computers or devices linked to your account.

Calendar Add an event

01 Open the app
Open the Calendar app and turn the iPad horizontal to see the dual-page layout. Navigate to the day you want and then tap the plus button on the bottom right.

02 Pop-up
An small pop-up window appears in the centre of the screen, as does the keyboard. Tap the field you wish to edit – such as Title – and then name your event.

03 Detail
You can add as much or as little detail as you want, including the location of the event. You have access to a full keyboard so you can go to town on the detail.

04 Time it
You now need to add the start and end date of your event, just to make sure you don't miss it! Tap on the relevant field to see the pop-up change into a new window display.

05 Familiar wheels
Use the wheels to select the times and dates that you want to use. You can also toggle the 'All-day' button instead if the event that is taking place will take up the entire day.

06 Done it
When you have everything in place, you need to tap the Done button located in the top-right corner of the window. Alternatively you can cancel it to return without saving.

07 Alert
Tap the Alert field to set reminders for the event. These will help ensure you don't miss an appointment. Alerts pop up on your iPad at the times you set them.

08 Tap it, save it
There are a number of options, ranging from at the event time to two hours before. Tap on the option you wish to use and a tick will appear. Save your progress by clicking Done.

09 Save and view
Save your event and then it will appear on the page. Tap on it to see the full details and to make changes. If you change your mind, tap the red 'Delete Event' button at the bottom.

App used:
Reminders

Time needed:
10 minutes

Never miss an event with Reminders

Thanks to Apple's new task management app, you have no excuse for forgetting birthdays

We all like to think that our minds operate like super-computers. As such, we utter the words, "Don't worry, I'll remember…" on an all-too regular basis, only to forget whatever it was we said we'd never forget. To help, Apple has now launched its own task management app as part of the iOS 5 update, and it's a cracker.

Reminders lets you organise your life into To Do lists, complete with due dates, notes and reminders to ensure that you never forget when something important is pressing. Simply jot down tasks, record when you need to do them by, then tick each one off as you complete it. Reminders is location-based, so if you need to pick up some groceries from the supermarket, you can be alerted as soon as you pull into the car park. The app also works with iCal, Outlook and iCloud, so any changes you make to your Reminders list will update automatically on all of your calendars. In this tutorial, we guide you through the process of setting your own reminders and managing your To Do lists.

"The Reminders app also works with iCal, Outlook and iCloud"

Reminders Setting yourself reminders

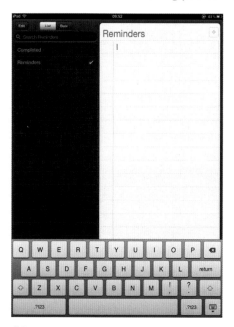

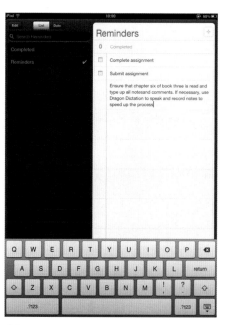

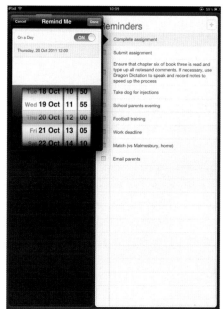

01 Add a reminder
You can immediately start compiling a To Do list by tapping either the paper, or the '+' button in the top-right corner. Use the default keyboard to type your reminder.

02 Make lists
Add reminders to your To Do list by tapping the page or the icon. The lines on the paper will even expand to neatly contain all of your text – just in case you have a complicated task to complete!

03 Add details
Tap a task to view your reminders. Tap Remind Me, slide 'On a Day' to On, then use the trusty wheels and hit the date to choose when your device should alert you.

Adding reminders

Never miss anything you had planned again!

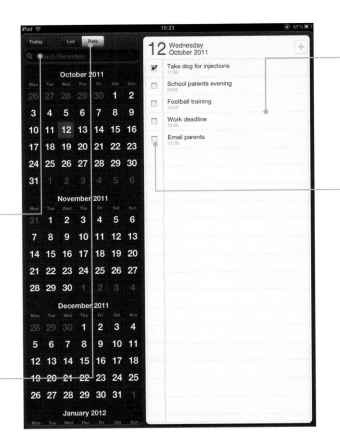

Search
If you end up with vast lists of reminders – both new and old – then you can search for a specific reminder by entering keywords into the search window

Tickboxes
Once you have successfully completed a task, place a tick in the box, and it will be removed from your reminders list and added to your 'completed' list for reference

Views
Your reminders can be viewed in a straightforward list, or on a day-to-day basis on the days you have set them for

Your system
By default, your tasks are arranged into Reminders or Completed sections. If you want to change the names of these categories or create new folders to store your reminders, tap the Edit button in the top-left corner, and then start creating new places for your filing system.

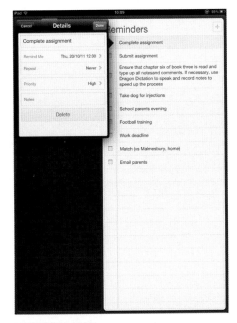

04 More options
You can set various other options, such as the priority, and add notes that relate to each task if you feel you may need more information. Tap Done when you're happy.

05 View as list or date
Your reminders can be categorised by the date. To assign reminders to a specific time period, tap Date, choose which one you wish to assign it to, then add it.

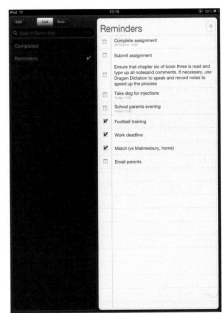

06 Tick them off
Whenever a task is completed, tap the box next to it to add a tick. Reminders that have been ticked will be added to your Completed list, making you feel good about yourself!

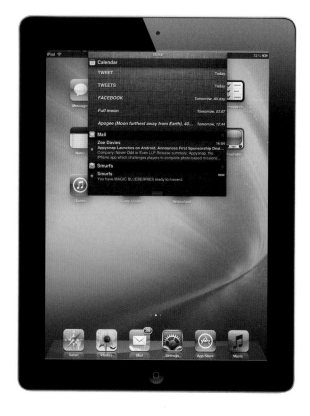

 **App used:**
Notification Center

 Time needed:
10 minutes

Customise your Notification Center

Make sure you never miss a thing by setting up your very own personalised Notification Center

Your iPad has always been good at notifying you about updates, messages, events and so on. In iOS 4, however, the way in which these messages were conveyed was intrusive, with a message box appearing in the middle of the screen. But iOS 5 embraces the concept of notifications, and the new system features an enhanced suite to allow you to tailor all aspects of how your device gets messages to you.

Now, you can get messages, notifications, news and the latest scores delivered to the top of your screen without disturbing what you're doing. All you have to do to set up your own personalised Notification Center is go to Settings, choose the apps, the order they appear in your Notification Center, and the manner in which they alert you. To stay in the loop, swipe down from the top of the screen, and you'll be presented with a list of notifications for all of the apps you have featured. Here, we show you how to get the most out of this great new feature.

"Tailor all aspects of how your device gets messages to you"

Notification Center How to set up and use your Notification Center

01 Go to Settings

From your iPad's Home screen, tap Settings, which is housed in your dock by default, then tap on Notifications, which should be the third option down on the list.

02 Adding items

In Settings, you can choose which apps are featured in Notification Center. Tap Edit, then hold the right-hand edge of each app strip, and drag it into position.

03 Tailoring notification options

Tap the arrow next to an app, and you will see options that are specific to that app. Choose how many items related to that app are displayed when a notification relating to it arrives.

Setting up your Notification Center

Tailoring the news feed that is all about you

View in Lock Screen
This option determines if alerts appear on your device's Lock Screen. It is good to have this activated so that you never miss a thing

Badge icons
This slider will determine whether the icon for the app that is notifying you is displayed in the alert. It looks better if they are on

Switch on
To get alerts for particular apps, ensure that the Notification Center slider is switch to On in each app you wish to see featured

Alert Style
You can decide how alerts are conveyed to you; either by the standard-style Alert, via a non-intrusive Banner, or no notifications at all

Sorting your apps
You can sort your apps on the Notification Center Settings screen by Time or Manually. Sorting by Time means that the order of alerts is based on the time they arrive. You can manually arrange the order of your Notifications by tapping Edit and then rearranging the apps by dragging them.

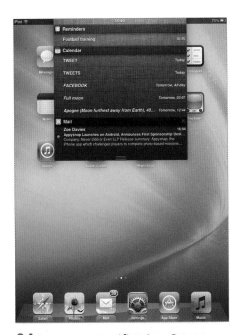

04 Accessing Notification Center

All you need to do is swipe down from the top of the screen to call up a window of notifications based on the options you have selected. If you liked the old boxes, you can select this option.

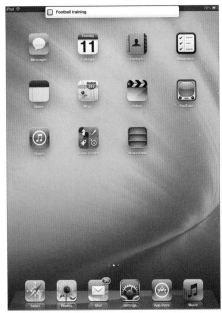

05 Your alerts

Notifications arrive in the form of a message at the top of the screen, and don't intrude with the app you are currently using, giving you the option to ignore it if you so wish.

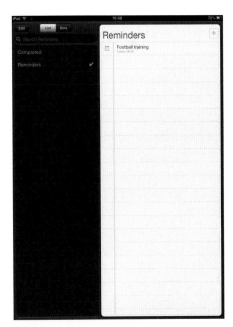

06 Go to app

If you need to respond to a notification immediately, tap it in your Notification Center, and you will be taken to the specific app to carry out your actions.

Add a contact

Add, store and update your contacts directly on your iPad

App used: Contacts **Time needed:** 10 minutes

Now that you've finally got your hands on a shiny new iPad, one of the first things you're going to want to do is add a contact to the sumptuous Contacts app. It works in much the same way as the app on the iPhone; it still has easy-to-find buttons and an intuitive natural feel but rather than having the screen shunt to the right through each menu, you get very nice pop-up boxes that are easy to use and make even more sense than the iPhone ever did. If you're new to the whole touch concept then this process will be a revelation in simplicity. Not only can you add all the pertinent information you need but there are cool little extras that make the system very slick and easy to use.

The Contacts app will work in both landscape and horizontal mode but we found that having all that screen real estate was suited better, in this instance, to the horizontal mode. The app is designed to look like an actual physical book and it gives the whole process a nice old-world feel. You can literally feel your way around all of the apps on the iPad and the contacts app is no different. Remember that even if you make a mistake you can go back and edit anything you like over and over again. You can also sync existing contacts from iTunes into the app.

"Contacts will work in both landscape and horizontal mode"

Detail
The book-like form and the attention to detail is incredible. You can even see the staples where the virtual book has been bound together

Edit
You can go back to any contact you want and edit their details by tapping on the Edit button at the very bottom of the page. It will take you back to the screen in step two

Contacts Add a people to your contacts

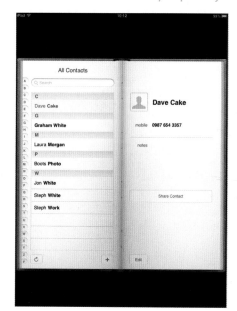

01 Open her up
Open the Contacts app from the home screen of your iPad and then use the '+' button, which can be found in the bottom right-hand side of the screen to begin adding the contact.

02 Tap and type
The keyboard will now appear and you can begin entering the necessary information. Tap on the field you wish to edit. A logical place to start is with the person's first name.

03 Cross it
As you type and get used to the keyboard you may make mistakes. You can use the backspace button to delete or remove everything using the little cross to the right of the field.

04 Add a photo

To add a photo just tap the add photo button and your photo albums (the ones you have synced) will magically appear. Tap on the one you wish to add from.

05 Take your pic

You can now choose from the pictures you have to hand. If there are more pictures than can fit in the pop-up window then you can scroll up and down in the window using a flick of the finger.

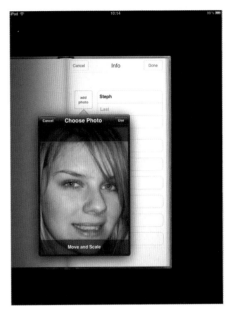

06 Move and scale

You now have to move and scale the picture you have selected. Those of you with an iPhone will be used to this. Use a pinch or reverse pinch to zoom in and out of the picture.

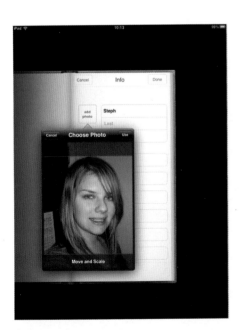

07 Use or cancel

Once the picture is how you would like it tap on the Use button on the top-right of the pop-up window. The picture you have selected will then slide into the photo area of the contact form.

08 Add fields

Go through the rest of the form and add as much or as little information as you need. Just tap into a field to edit it and the keyboard will spring up from the bottom of the screen.

09 Done

Once you are completely finished all you need to do is hit the Done button in the top-right of the page to save the changes and then simply return to the address book.

App used:
FaceTime

 Time needed:
10 minutes

Manage your contacts in FaceTime

If you want to make a call you have to know how to access your contacts. Here's how to add new details and delete others while managing your FaceTime contacts

The first time you use FaceTime it might be surprising to see that the Contacts section is fully populated. It's because FaceTime uses the details in the Contacts app and this in turn can import all the contacts that you have in Outlook or Address Book. Each time there's a sync with iTunes, the contacts are synchronised across all the apps. If you don't use Outlook or Address Book then – of course – the people in the Contacts folder will just be the ones you've added.

It isn't necessary to add or delete anything using FaceTime; you can do it in the Contacts app. As soon as anything is changed here it is reflected in the FaceTime app. Any changes will then be propagated back to the desktop program you are syncing contacts with to ensure conformity across all the software. Equally, any change to a contact in FaceTime is reflected in Contacts and then transferred back when syncing. In this tutorial though, we're going to import contacts from Outlook and manage them from within FaceTime.

"FaceTime can import all the contacts that you have in Outlook or Address Book"

FaceTime Managing your contacts

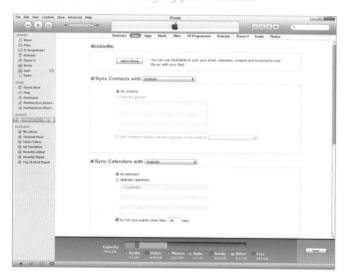

01 Import contacts

Go to iTunes while performing a wireless sync. Click on your device in the pane. Click Info on the menu above the main screen. Now put a tick in the box that says 'Sync Contacts with' and select Outlook. This should populate your FaceTime contacts.

02 Delete old contacts

Perform a sync to add your Outlook contacts to both Contacts and FaceTime. Tap on FaceTime and then Contacts. To delete a contact that you won't be needing any more, tap on the name of it, then Edit. Scroll to the bottom and tap Delete Contact.

Storing the details

Add images, input details or delete old contacts entirely

Add an image
To give your contacts a more visual look tap on the Add Photo button and either use the camera to take a picture or browse the Photo Library for one. You can scale the image to fit the square

Change the tune
By default, all contacts will ring you with the same built-in ringtone which is the Strum noise. However, you can change this to any of the alarm noises by tapping on Ringtone

Remove details
To change the entry for a field just tap on it and edit it. However, to remove it completely without editing or replacement, tap on the red dash by the side on any entry

Adding favourites
If you have a lot of contacts and most of them aren't on FaceTime then it makes sense to sort them out using the Favorites button. Either add people to Favorites when looking at their details, or, if looking at the Favorites list, tap on the Plus sign and scroll through the contacts list.

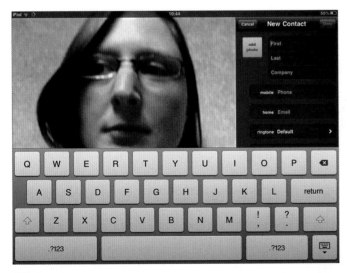

03 Add new contacts

To add a new contact tap on the '+' symbol, located in the top right of the FaceTime interface. Enter all the details you have to hand then click on Add Photo. Select to either take a photo or choose one from the Library. Once you've completed this click on Done.

04 Share your contacts

To share a contact with someone else, select the contact in question and then tap on Share Contact. Type in the email address of the person to share the contact with, write your message and click on Send. All the contact details will now be emailed to that person.

App used:
FaceTime

Time needed:
10 minutes

Make calls using FaceTime

It's one of the most exciting features of the iPad 2, the ability to make video calls. Here's how you sign up and then call someone for a video conversation

 The addition of dual cameras to the iPad 2 was one of the worst kept secrets yet most anticipated features of the device's launch. Not so much for the ability to go out and take pictures with your iPad, but for video calling and video capture and transmission.

Yes, FaceTime arrived on the iPad 2 and it had its very own app. If you're used to an iPhone where FaceTime is built in to the phone app then this is slightly different. The cameras are the same resolution, so if you think your main screen image looks soft, it's because it's being displayed at the huge iPad size, not a tiny iPod touch screen size.

The first thing you need to have in place before any calls are made is to register FaceTime using your Apple ID. This is the ID that is used by Apple and the App Store for purchases. Once the Apple ID is set up for the FaceTime account then an email address needs to be assigned to it. This is the one that you will use to call other people and that they will use to call you.

"Before any calls are made, you must register FaceTime using your Apple ID"

FaceTime Register FaceTime and make calls

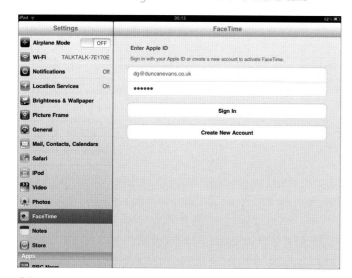

01 Register your details

To register your details, tap on the Settings app and scroll down the list of built-in apps until you get to FaceTime. Tap on this and toggle FaceTime On. You will be required to enter your Apple ID. Enter the email address and the password and then tap on Sign In to get started.

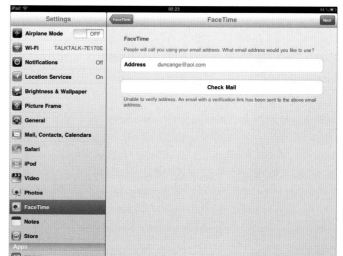

02 Select an address

FaceTime can use different email addresses. Enter the one that you would like to use for your calls. If it's the same as your Apple ID account, it will be verified immediately. However, if it is a different email address, a verification link will be sent to that address.

Making a call

It's easy to make FaceTime calls. Just find your contacts who actually use it and call away

Cameras in use
When activating FaceTime for a call, the first thing you see is yourself. When FaceTime connects the call, this window shrinks to a postage size so you can still see yourself and this main window fills with the video from the contact

Making contact
The names in this list aren't ones you've logged as FaceTime users, it's everyone in your Contacts database. Tap on a name to see if they have a FaceTime email you can use

People in touch
The list of Recent calls covers both those ringing you and you ringing them. If it's a frequent contact you want to call, it's quicker to tap here than to scroll through the entire contacts list for someone's details

Dual cameras
The real advantage of having front and rear-facing cameras in a FaceTime call is that either the person calling or the one receiving, or both, can turn the other camera on and show the other person something that is going on in front of them. All you need to do is tap the camera symbol with the rotating arms to switch your camera from front facing to rear facing.

03 Get into FaceTime

Once verified, your details will be displayed and FaceTime will be on. Exit Settings and tap on the FaceTime app. This will show the display from the front-facing camera. Then simply tap on the Contacts box found at the bottom in order to list them.

04 Make a call

Tap on the person whom you would like to call. If they have a FaceTime account the email address will be shown with a blue video camera icon next to it. Tap on the email address in order to make the call. This will then telephone the contact.

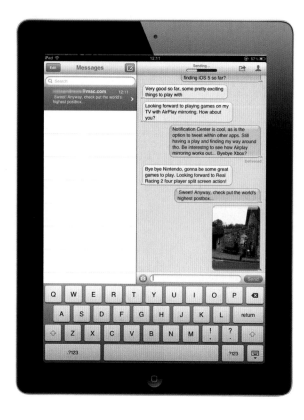

App used:
iMessage

Time needed:
5 minutes

Keep in contact with friends using iMessage

Get to grips with Apple's new messaging service and send unlimited text messages to your friends

With iOS 5, it has never been easier to stay in touch with your friends and family using your Apple device. Thanks to iMessage, you can send unlimited text messages to everyone you know over Wi-Fi or 3G.

The app works exactly like the iPhone Messages app, letting you share photos, videos, locations and contacts around your social circles, and keep everyone in the loop via group messaging. To start, tap the 'New Message' button, and enter the mac addresses of the people you wish to contact. Then simply enter words into a text field, hitting the camera button to attach media, and tapping the Send button. The interface is fabulously intuitive. It's free, so as long as your friends have iOS 5 installed, you can text without worrying about incurring a hefty bill. All messages can be tracked with delivery receipts, and thanks to the iCloud, you can start a conversation on one device, and finish it later on another. In this tutorial, we guide you through the process of using iMessage for the first time…

"It's never been easier to stay in touch with your friends and family"

---

iMessage How to text for free

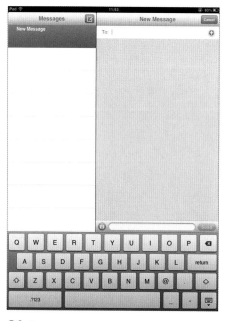

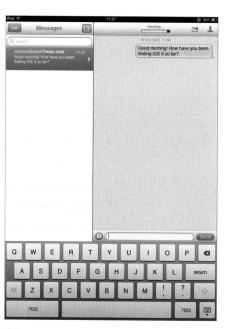

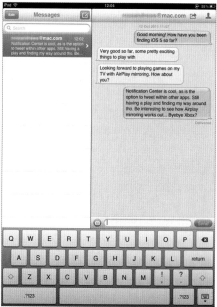

01 Create a message

To kick things off you will need to tap the 'New Message' icon, and you'll be prompted to enter the mac address of the person you wish to send a message to.

02 Type and send

Tap on the text field, and type your message into the window. When you have finished writing what you wish to say, hit Send, and your message will be delivered.

03 Quick conversations

The conversations will be neatly displayed in the main window, and the text will be colour-coded so you know who said what – blue will be your message and grey the recipient.

Free and easy messaging

Quickly conversing has never been so easy

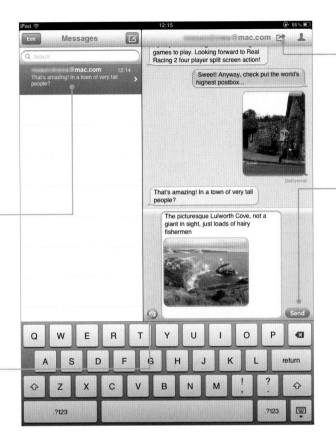

Delete messages
Delete messages by tapping the arrow icon at the top of the window and then individually selecting messages to erase

Instant messaging
Sending messages is easy; just tap on the text field, type what you want, and hit the Send button. Each text bubble is colour-coded to make it easy to see who said what

Your recipients
All of your friends will be listed in the column to the left of the window. You can bring in more people for group conversations

Adding photos
Images and videos can be added and attached to your messages. Just type your message, and then tap the camera icon to select and send media

Adding contacts
All of your Apple apps work well together. You can add contacts from iMessage to your Contacts app by tapping on the portrait icon at the top of the screen while in iMessage, and then entering the person's details into the contact page that appears.

04 Adding images
Once you have typed your message, tap the camera icon, pick a photograph you wish to send from your Camera Roll, and then tap Use to include it in your next message.

05 Notifications
iMessage works alongside your Notification Center, so if you receive any new messages you will be instantly notified and can then be taken straight to the app to reply.

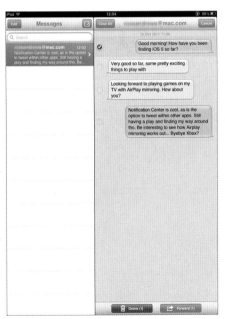

06 Deleting messages
If there are parts of conversations you want to delete, tap the arrow in the top-right corner, and tick the circle next to the message. This will help you keep track of the important parts.

App used:
Notes

Time needed:
5 minutes

Make notes on your iPad

Don't feel you need to purchase Pages in order to jot down ideas on your iPad – you can do this just as easily with the built-in Notes app

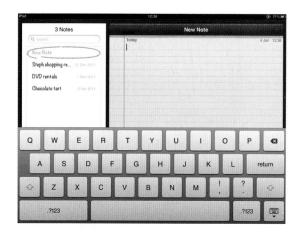

Despite the fact that some people view the iPad as a device designed merely to consume media, just spending a few minutes with it will make you realise that this isn't true. With the help of a few choice programs, the iPad is capable of being used to create drawings, edit photos or write essays. But you don't need to purchase anything for the latter, as the Notes app comes bundled with the iPad and is a really great place to start exploring how you can handle typing on glass.

Notes is remarkably similar to the program bearing the same name on the iPhone and iPod touch, it has simply been expanded a little to take advantage of the additional space the iPad screen provides. This step-by-step tutorial will show you how it works, what you can do with it, and how it could help you in your day-to-day activities.

> "Notes comes bundled with the iPad and is a great place to start exploring how you can handle typing on glass"

Notes app on iPad

The Notes app is great for jotting down ideas on the go, and even copying text from the web to read later…

Swipe
You don't have to select a note to delete it, just swipe its title to reveal this Delete button – just like the messages in Mail

Add
You can add as many notes as you need. Whether you're in the landscape or portrait orientation, this button is always top-right of the screen

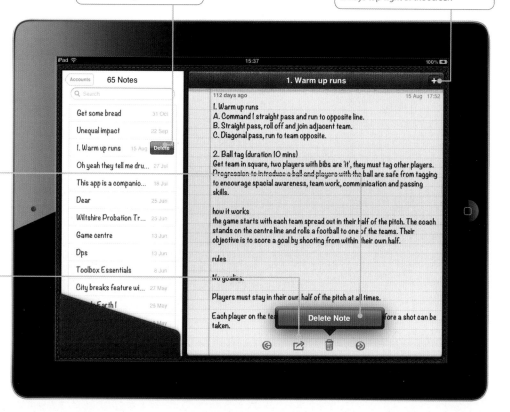

Delete
If you no longer need a particular note, select it and tap on this button. You'll be asked to confirm your choice just in case you tapped on it by mistake

Emailing
Notes lets you email the content of your pages without you having to copy and paste the information yourself. Tap on this icon to create an email message

Text, but no images
You could use Notes to keep information from the web so you can read it when you don't have access to Wi-Fi. The iPad's copy and paste system works perfectly for this, but be aware that it only lets you copy text – you can't add images to Notes.

Notes Use Notes to write down ideas

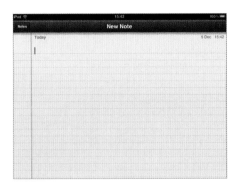

01 The look of Notes

Hold your iPad in the portrait orientation and tap the Notes app. Tap on the screen to reveal the keyboard. Now you can begin typing your very first note.

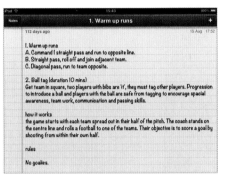

02 The '+' button

When you have finished, tap on the keyboard symbol with the down arrow (bottom-right of the keyboard) to dismiss it, then tap on the '+' button in the top-right of the interface.

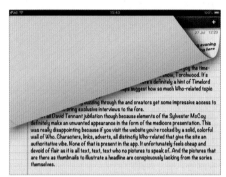

03 From one to another

That last action created a brand-new note. You can swap between the first one and the one you're currently working on by tapping on the arrow buttons.

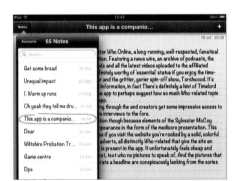

04 Pop-up menu

If you want to see all the pages you have created, tap on the Notes button to reveal a pop-up menu. They are presented in the chronological order you created them.

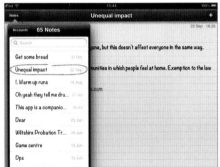

05 The selected note

Whichever note is currently selected has a big red circle around its title. You can swipe down to reveal more notes, if you have them stored on your device.

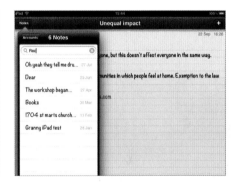

06 Searching

There's also a search field at the very top of the pop-up menu, which can help you narrow down your search when you happen to be looking for any specific information.

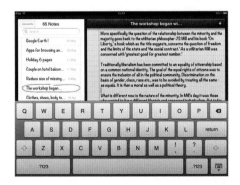

07 Landscape

Turn the iPad to the landscape orientation. The notes don't get any wider, but your list becomes permanently available on the left-hand side for easy accessibility.

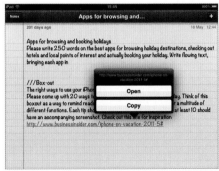

08 Tappable links

If you type in a web link, it'll become active as soon as you hide the keyboard. Tap on it and you'll be sent to Safari. Tapping an email address sends you to Mail.

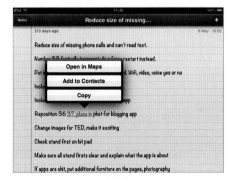

09 Save numbers

Your iPad also recognises phone numbers. Since you can't phone people, you're offered two other options: to Create New Contact or Add To Existing Contact. For places you can Open in Maps.

 App used:
Maps

 Time needed:
5 minutes

Save a bookmark in Maps

Save your favourite places and locations easily in Apple's built-in Maps application

The Maps app is a useful addition on the iPhone and one that we've used countless times, but for some reason it hadn't really registered as a big deal on the iPad. That was until we loaded it and saw just how incredible it is on the huge iPad screen and how the Apple engineers have made the same technology so snappy and responsive. The way the maps render so much quicker is one of the clearest ways we've found to compare the processing power of the iPad versus the iPhone. With this in mind, it's useful to know how to quickly search for items and save them so that they can be called upon at any time. This iPad Maps app is very simple to use and has some very cool detailing, which would have gone unnoticed on the smaller iPhone screen. The only drawback on the Wi-Fi-only iPad is that it's not a great portable app.

"You can quickly search for items and save them so that they can be called upon at any time"

Maps Adding a location bookmark

01 Load it, tap it
Load Maps from your home screen and begin your search by tapping your finger on the address/location field at the top of the interface. Type it in or search for your current location.

02 Type it, watch it
Once you've typed in your place and hit the search button, a pin will drop in the location. This should happen with satisfying speed. Above the pin the location should be named.

03 View change
You can change the view of the location in question by activating the hidden menu. To do this, use your finger to curl back the right-hand corner of the map. Tap on a view option.

Maps on the big screen

Maps makes full use of the large screen by throwing pop-up windows of information

Toggle it
On the top left of the interface is the toggle switch between the search function and the directions function. Like the iPhone version, Maps on the iPad can act as a sat-nav system

Cool clarity
The full zoom on the Maps app lets you see the planet in really stunning detail. The speed with which this app can do this only adds to the mesmerising nature of the experience

My location, different location
The 'My Location' button is situated at the top of the app window in the iPad version. Tap it to have your own location triangulated automatically

Super speed
The speed of the Maps app comes down to the Apple-made A4 processor and the RAM chip it's connected to working together to make a much snappier experience. The maps render much faster than on the iPhone.

04 Zoom it
Use a pinch or reverse pinch to zoom in and out of the map so you can get an idea of what surrounds the location. You could be looking for nearby tube stations or bus stops, for example.

05 Closer look
You can also get in nice and close to your location and see exactly what it looks like. To begin adding it as a bookmark you need to hit the 'i' button next to the tag.

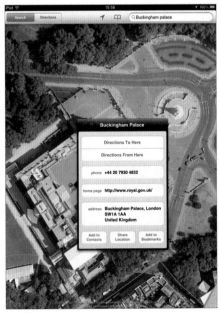

06 Roomy view
The info box will now spring up and you can use the button at the bottom to add the location to your Maps bookmarks. This process can be repeated for every location you want to add.

App used:
Maps

Time needed:
10 minutes

Get directions using Maps

One of the most prominent features of the Maps application is directions. You can get directions between any two locations or nearby places with a few simple taps

 The Maps application on the iPad is more usable than it is on the smaller devices as there's a lot less scrolling involved. Things like Traffic and Street View look brilliant on the larger screen, and Maps also has a new Terrain view that adds a layer of topographical data to the maps.

Maps on the iPad can be used to get directions between two places. It pulls out a lot of useful information related to a route that is very useful for a commuter, such as Driving/Transit/Walking Directions, Distance and Time to Commute. When using Transit Directions it also shows you the Transit Timings to help you plan ahead. You can also make use of the Traffic information when using directions, which will help you avoid unwanted delays. Google Street View gives a panoramic view of the destination, but note that this is not available on all the locations. The locations where it is available are indicated by the Street View icon. Follow our tutorial to discover just how easy it is to get directions on your iPad and follow them with no hassle at all.

"Things like Traffic and Street View look brilliant on the larger screen"

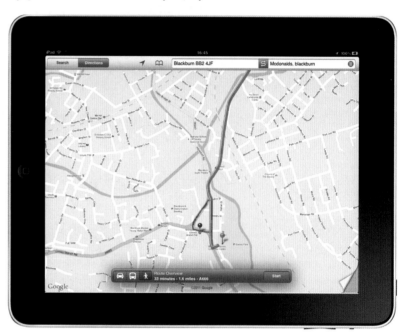

Maps Get directions using Maps

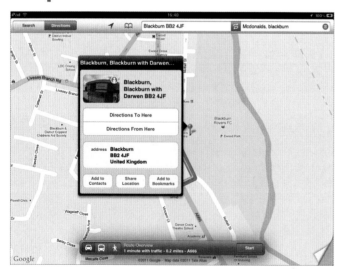

01 Set the Start Address
Search for a location on the map or, if you want to start from the current location, tap the My Location button in the bottom-left of the screen. Tap the pin to bring up the pop-up menu, and choose Directions From Here. Tap Directions, then enter the address. Now tap Search.

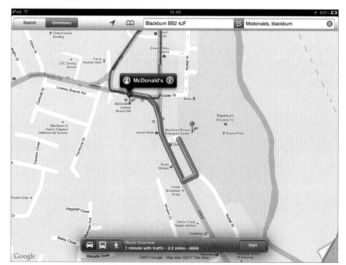

02 Set the destination address
Enter the destination in the End box. If there are multiple addresses, Maps will put red pins for all the searched locations. The green pin is connected by a blue line to a red pin. The green pin represents your start location, the blue line represents the route and the red pin represents the destination.

Get directions on your iPad

Use the Maps app to reach your destination

Current location
Locate the current address with the help of any of the available GPS technologies

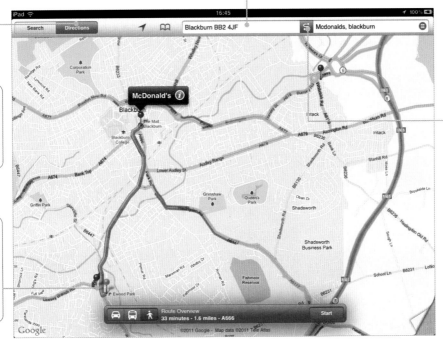

Bookmarks/ Recents/Contacts
Access Map Bookmarks, Recent Location Searches and Contacts here

Reverse directions
Reverse the searched route by simply tapping the wiggly arrow icon between the two locations

Start and destination locations
Green pins represent the start locations and red pins represent the destinations

GPS technology on iPad Wi-Fi and 3G
iPad Wi-Fi is an inferior GPS device when compared to iPad 3G. Wi-Fi depends on Skyhook Wireless Wi-Fi-based GPS technology to provide basic location specific data. Therefore it cannot be used where accurate GPS data is required. iPad 3G uses GSM and A-GPS in addition to Skyhook Wireless to determine location-specific information instead.

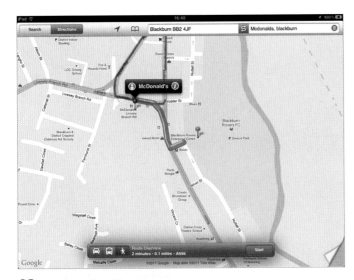

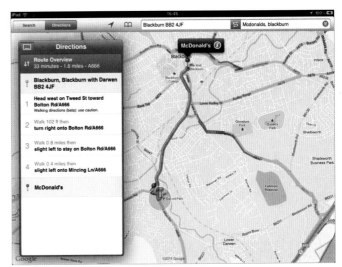

03 Getting the directions

Select the method of commute by tapping one of the icons in the top left-hand corner of the map. The options are for road, public transport or on foot. When a method is selected, the route map, the applicable distance and the expected time to reach your destination will be updated automatically.

04 View turn-by-turn directions

Tap Start to view the turn-by-turn directions. Upon tapping Start you will get the driving directions on the blue bar. You can navigate through turn-by-turn directions using a swipe of a finger. Directions will indicate turns and distances so you can be sure you get the right one each time.

App used:
Maps

Time needed:
10 minutes

Send and receive locations with Maps

The excellent Maps application on the iPad makes it very easy to share your location and receive information showing you where other people are

The Maps application on the iOS platform is much more than just a map. It provides a wide range of things to do around maps, such as finding a route, studying geographical information, viewing real-time traffic information, viewing traffic, street views and much more besides. Among these there is a feature that is exceptionally useful called Share Location. To portray the usefulness of this little feature, let's say that while driving around you have discovered a cave of treasure. So you think you need to take it all now otherwise somebody else might discover it. What will you do? You will open your iPad, find out the current location and then send an email with directions to the cave (using the Share Location feature), that's what.

In this step-by-step tutorial we will show you exactly how to share your location using the Maps app, so that you never miss an opportunity – especially one as big as this. Okay, so this kind of epic event won't happen to you all the time, but there are plenty of other occasions when rather than giving someone convoluted directions, you can just share your location easily using this method. It's pretty easy, and here we show you how…

"There is a feature that is useful called Share Location"

Maps   Use the Maps app to let others know where you are

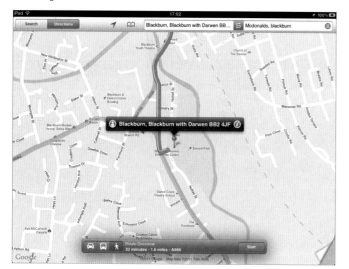

01 Locating the address

To begin, you need to locate the address you want to share. You can do this by searching your location in the search box or by dropping a pin on the location you want to share. A box will appear containing your location on screen.

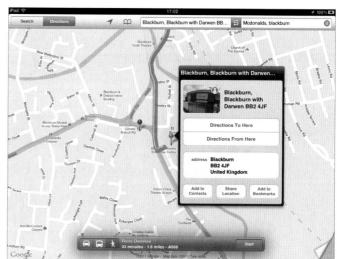

02 Sharing the location

Once you have the correct location, tap on the pin to bring up the detailed information in a pop-up box. Tap the Share Location button available at the bottom of the window (you can also add the address to your contacts or bookmarks from here).

Use Maps to show friends where you are
Send your current location to friends via email

Where it's at
Once you've tapped the current location button your location will appear as a green dot with a blue ring around it

Me
Tap this button to see your own location. You'll need to be connected to the internet either through Wi-Fi or using a 3G SIM, if you are a 3G iPad owner

Pick a pin
Tap on any pin and you will see an information window which will allow you to share the location with anyone you like

Map type
Here we are using a standard Map but you can use a satellite image, or a hybrid that shows satellite imagery overlaid with map info like road and place names

VCF file
'.vcf' is the extension of a file used to store electronic business cards in the vCard format. A 'vcf' file may contain name and address info, phone numbers, email addresses, URLs, logos, photos, and audio clips. 'vcf' or vCard format is popular to share contact info on the internet or between devices. Other standards for sharing contact info is hCard and Internet Business Card.

03 Sending the location
Type in the email address of the person you want to share your location with. Email is already populated with important information such as the location (in the form of a 'vcf' file) and the location's name as the subject and body. Tap Send to send the location to the recipient.

04 Using the Shared Location
Open the email with the 'vcf' file attached in it. Tap on it to open the information pop-up. It is similar to one you have seen in the Maps application, but it contains more information. It also contains the Map URL. Tap on Map URL to launch the Maps app with the sent address.

App used:
App Store

 Time needed:
5 minutes

Use the App Store on your iPad

One of the best things about your iPad is that it can be upgraded on the go. The App Store allows you to make the iPad even more magical than it already is…

The iPad is magical, and a major part of the magic is that you can expand its capabilities with cheap or even free apps. The App Store has been a roaring success for Apple, with over 400,000 applications to choose from – not to mention the 1 billion Dollars that it's made for developers.

The number and range of applications on offer is quite stunning. The App Store has applications to help you plan large projects, word processors, web browsers; the list is endless. The software tends to be incredibly good value too – it's amazing what your iPad can do with just a 69p investment. The fact that the App Store is right there on your iPad means that you can buy stuff on the go, too, and download apps directly onto the device.

With so much choice it can be quite difficult to discover exactly what you want, but the App Store on the iPad is easy enough to use when you know how, so follow these simple steps to learn more…

"It's amazing what your iPad can do with just a 69p investment"

Navigate the App Store on your iPad

Find and download iPad apps

Latest apps
Find out what applications have just hit the App Store by tapping on the Release Date button. This will show you the very latest approved apps

Search
Find exactly what you need by tapping in the search box and typing. Suggestions will automatically drop-down as you type – simply tap on them to jump to those results

Featured
The default screen on the App Store shows off some of the best applications available in a Cover Flow style – simply swipe left and right to see what's there

Navigation
Get to the charts and categories sections here by tapping on the relevant icons. If Updates has a red icon with a number in it, upgrades are ready to be downloaded

App Store Learn how to use the App Store on your iPad

01 Getting started

Once you've set up an account, simply tap the App Store icon to get started. The first screen you see has some of the most interesting apps as defined by Apple.

02 Staff Picks

If you'd like to see what the staff at Apple are interested in and using the most, scroll down with a swipe to the Staff Favourites. Tap See All to view them all.

03 App of the week

Each week a new app is chosen to be the app of the week. These are often surprising and it's a great way to find a really good app you might not have seen.

04 Find apps

If you know the name of the app you want, simply tap in the search field and type it there. If you're not sure just put the type of application to find what you need.

05 Charts

Apple lets you see the top ten selling apps and the top ten free ones. Simply tap on the Top Charts button at the bottom of the screen to see what they are.

06 What's hot

The What's Hot section lists some of the best apps that might not have made it to the charts or have been featured yet. Tap What's Hot at the top of the Store.

07 Categories

If you're not sure what you want but have a general idea, tap the Categories button. This shows twenty different groups for apps to narrow down your choice.

08 Buying an app

When you're ready to buy an app, getting it is really simple. Tap on the price and it will change to 'Buy App'. Tap again and then enter your account password.

09 Updating an app

Over time, and more regularly than you might imagine, apps will be updated. Tap on Updates and then either Update All or pick applications to update individually.

App used:
iTunes

 Time needed:
10 minutes

Navigate iTunes on your iPad

You can download all your favourite movies and music from iTunes
without needing to connect it to your computer

Being able to download music and movies on the go is one of the best things about the iPad. With the enormous selection available on the iTunes Store, you're unlikely to be lost for something to suit your mood. It's not just music and movies though, as you can also download TV programmes, audio books and podcasts. There's even the iTunes U section, which is full of education resources.

Your purchases are automatically synced and pushed to all of your devices wirelessly via iCloud, so you always have full access to your purchase history, wherever you are. This means that you'll be able to watch your movies on your computer or Apple TV and, more importantly, that you'll have a guaranteed backup of everything you purchase.

To use iTunes on the iPad you'll need an account to get going, but once that's set up you can buy songs, apps or movies wherever you are, all you need is a credit card (or, failing that, some iTunes gift cards).

"You can buy songs, apps or movies wherever you are with ease"

Navigate the iTunes Store on your iPad

Download songs and movies direct to your device

Featured, Charts, Genius
To see what the bestselling items are tap on the Top Charts button, or to see suggestions based on your purchasing history and iTunes library tap Genius

Search
Find everything you're after by tapping in the search box and typing. iTunes will automatically suggest what it thinks you're after. To select one, just tap it

Latest content
The very latest releases and some of the more popular content is automatically displayed. You can see more by tapping on the arrows at each corner of the section

Easy access
To get to a specific section quickly simply tap on the relevant icon along the bottom of the screen. This narrows down the amount of searching you have to do

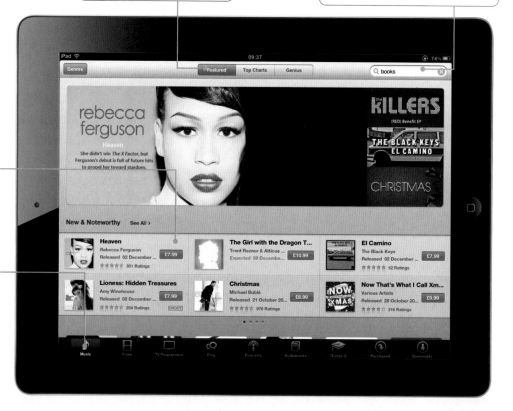

iTunes Discover how to download music and movies

01 Buy music, movies and more

In order to buy music and videos from the iTunes Store you'll need to set up an account. Tap on an item to buy it and then choose the Create New Account option.

02 Terms and conditions

There are a few steps to opening a new account on the iPad. Once you've tapped to confirm your location you'll then be offered the terms and conditions for using the account.

03 Credit card details

You'll need to provide your credit card details in order to purchase items. If you don't want to do this, simply buy an iTunes gift card and enter the number here.

04 Search

To search for your favourite music, video and television programmes, tap in the search box. The on-screen keyboard will appear so you can type your entry.

05 Music, Video, TV

To see what's just been added or the latest promotions, just tap on the Music, Films and TV Programmes icons along the bottom of the screen.

06 Charts

The most popular content in each of the sections is on the Charts page. There are charts pages for everything, including podcasts, video, television and music.

07 Genius

If you have bought from the Store before, tap on the Genius button to see recommendations based on the content of your library – this is a good way to find a hot new band.

08 Other offers

On the main screen it's easy to be lured in by the flashy graphics, but scroll down and you'll see further offers such as free content, cheap music and current offers.

09 Monitor downloads

When you've made a purchase in iTunes you can see how long it's likely going to take by tapping on the Downloads icon in the bottom-right of the screen.

 App used:
iTunes

 Time needed:
10 minutes

Use iTunes to download media

We show you how to use Apple's virtual superstore to purchase music, films and other assorted media

 The birth of iTunes signalled a significant change in the way we shop for music and media. Everything can now be bought whenever and wherever we are and it's all thanks to iTunes.

The iTunes app for your iPad is a friendly and welcoming portal to a thriving online marketplace where you can shop at your leisure and not be suckered into slinging cheap tat that is on display next to the tills into your basket. You go in, get what you want and, within minutes, be listening to it through your iPad's Music app or watching it through the Videos app. Using iTunes really couldn't be easier. Everything is well laid out and easily accessible and all of your past and present purchases are with you at all times for when you need them. The hardest part, if there even is a hard part, is ensuring that all of your billing information is up-to-date and correct. Once it is, all of the sonics and flicks you could ever want will be at your fingertips. Here we guide you through this essential app.

"iTunes is a friendly and welcoming portal to a thriving online marketplace"

iTunes How to browse and buy media

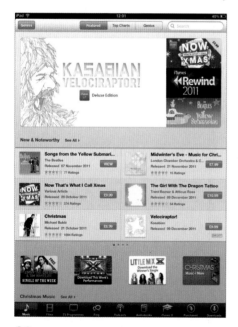

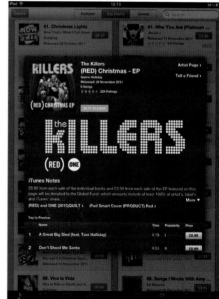

01 Launch iTunes

When you launch the iTunes app you will be taken straight to the main storefront, which is the Music Store by default. All of the categories in the store are laid out across the bottom of the screen.

02 Browse the store

The newest, most exciting media will always be displayed on the main page. If you don't find what you want there then you can search for artists and albums by using the 'Search' window.

03 Purchase music

When you find what you want, tap on it to bring up a window. Then tap the price at the top to buy the entire album, or tap on the price next to the separate tracks to download them individually.

Exploring the iTunes app

Navigating the user-friendly interface

Search for content
You can use the 'Featured', 'Top Charts' and 'Genius' tabs to find media, or you can enter specific keywords into the Search engine to instantly find what you want

Featured content
All of the most recent, hottest releases will be displayed in the main 'Featured' window that appears when you first tap on each store section

Downloads
When you purchase a song, film or other media from iTunes, they will be sent to the Downloads section where you can see their download progress by tapping on this icon here

Store categories
All of the different store categories, such as Music, Films, TV Shows, etc, are displayed as icons along the bottom of the screen. Tap on one to access it

Get past purchases
With iCloud integration, it isn't just your current purchases that are pushed to your other iOS 5 devices. A new section in the iTunes app, called 'Purchased' will allow you to view all media downloaded through your Apple ID and allow you to instantly download it again onto your current device.

04 Authorise download

After opting to download an item you will be required to sign in using your Apple ID to authorise the purchase. You may also be required to enter billing information.

05 Buy more media

You can also purchase films, TV shows, podcasts, audiobooks and educational materials through iTunes. The main difference being that with movies you can choose to rent, as well as buy.

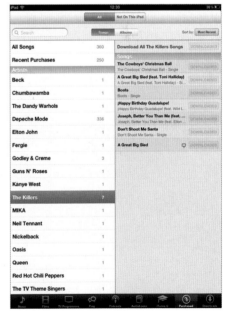

06 iTunes in the Cloud

The iTunes app is compatible with your personal iCloud, which means that anything you purchase from the store will be automatically pushed to all of your other iOS 5 devices free of charge.

The next step

132
Presentations via iPad

134
Stream with AirPlay

138
Print from your iPad

140
Twitter made simple

Get to grips with the iPad's more in-depth features with our guides

"Keynote lets you create presentations wherever you are without the binding need for wires"

The next step

 App used:
Camera

 Time needed:
5 minutes

Take faster photos on your iPad 2

Use the abilities of the iPad 2 to take great photos faster using the volume button

While the iPad 2 has been able to take photos since its launch, the only technique to use up until now has been a tap of the screen to take your snap. Sadly, due to the size of the device, touching the centre of the screen while holding it up is a little difficult and can lead to hand shake and motion blur in your shots. Luckily, though, there is now a way around this issue.

iOS 5 has brought with it several new and useful abilities inside the Camera app, all of which make taking and viewing your photos a lot quicker and easier. By far the most useful feature, though, is the option to take a snapshot with the 'Volume Up' button on the side of your device. It's quick, easy and most of all it's comfortable to reach when holding the iPad up to take your photo, making this one of the best additions to iOS 5 that Apple has introduced.

However, that isn't the end of it – viewing your photos is even easier thanks to a new way to access your Camera Roll, simply by swiping across the screen. And now you can even edit your photos on the iPad 2 as soon as you've taken them, ensuring that even a skewed shot can be straightened out, right on your iPad 2. In this guide we take you through all the key new features iOS 5 has to offer.

Camera Take incredible photos

01 The screen

In the Camera app, you'll see a shutter button in the centre of the bottom bar, and two buttons at the top to change the camera direction and the settings you are using.

02 Zooming in and out

In iOS 5 the gesture for zooming with the camera has changed to become more natural. You can now pinch in and out with two fingers, just as you do to zoom in on other apps.

03 Video recording

You can tap the toggle at the bottom right of the screen to switch between photo and movie mode. The camera records 720p video, so it's of a good quality.

Taking a fast snapshot

Make the most of
the Camera app

Volume button
Tapping the volume button on the top right of your iPad will allow you to take a photograph without even touching the screen

Options
Unlike the iPhone 4S, which has an LED flash option, your choice here is limited to adding gridlines to the screen while you shoot

Tap to expose
You can tap anywhere on the screen to make a small focus square appear. It sets the focus on the item you tapped and alters the lighting of the scene

Access to library
New in iOS 5 is the ability to access your Camera Roll without carefully tapping the icon in the bottom left. Simply swipe from the left edge

Photo editing
When you've taken a shot, you can edit the photo right on your iPad 2 by choosing the Edit button when viewing your photos. This will give you options to Enhance, Straighten, Crop and Rotate your shot, as well as giving you the chance to remove red-eye from your shots.

04 Gridlines
If you want to line up your shots perfectly, turn Gridlines on by tapping the Options button at the top of the screen and swiping the slider to 'On'. This will help you when composing your shots.

05 Face the front
The front-facing camera on the iPad 2 isn't just for FaceTime – it can also be used to take snapshots too. Just tap the icon in the top right of the screen and take the photo with the volume up button.

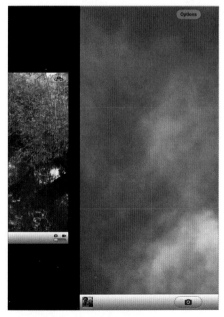

06 View your shots
If you tap the tiny image at the bottom left you'll view your Camera Roll, but in iOS 5 you can also just swipe from the left edge of the screen to view it quickly.

The next step

Editing images using Photos

To get the most from your iPad 2 camera, you can take advantage of the new iOS 5 photo editing feature

The introduction of iOS 5 has brought over 200 new features to the table. One is the ability for iPad 2 users to edit photos directly on the device in the Photos app. The editing software isn't going to turn you into David Bailey or your photos into works of art, yet it does help to enhance photos that have been taken with the camera or those you have copied onto the tablet.

The editing features available include the ability to rotate images from portrait to landscape. There's also an enhance option which can adjust the colour depth, brightness and contrast. The last few options should prove useful as well; the first of these is to remove the notorious red-eye that you get in photos which have been overloaded with flash. The ability to crop images also helps when you only want a specific part of a photo and want to remove the rest.

For this tutorial you will have needed to upgrade your iPad 2 to the latest iOS 5 firmware and we assume that you know how to get photos onto the tablet, either from email attachments, iTunes syncing or directly from the camera itself – there are guides to completing these tasks elsewhere in the book if necessary. Otherwise the tutorial should be fairly easy to follow.

Photos Editing photos on your iPad 2

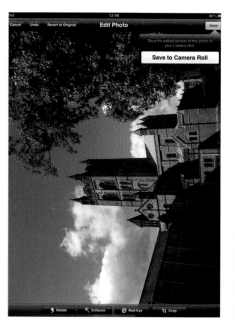

01 Selecting your photo

Launch the Photos app from your home screen, select the Photos or Albums tab at the top, then tap on the photo you want to adjust. Click Edit from the top-right of the screen.

02 Rotate photo

Select the Rotate option at the base and keep clicking it to rotate the photo if it's in the wrong orientation. When you are done, click Save or 'Save to Camera Roll' when prompted.

03 Enhance image

Edit an image and then click on Enhance at the bottom. Watch as the software adjusts the image. Re-press Enhance to turn off the effect or click Save to finish.

Editing interface

Editing your photos is as intuitive as the iPad 2 itself

Multi-touch controls
Before you choose how to edit a photo, you can use the multi-touch pinch controls to zoom into the photo to pick up on the areas you want to improve

Enhance
On the surface this seems like a basic option compared to most dedicated editing packages, but in practice it's a great feature that can transform your photo within moments

Undo any changes
Thanks to the intuitiveness of the iPad 2, you can easily undo any mistakes or revert back to the original image and then quickly re-save it

Crop photos
Crop is another underestimated feature. With Crop in action you can chop out parts of the photo (could be a blurred section) that you don't want any more

Forward photo
Once you have made changes to your photo you can use the Forward option (top-right corner) to assign the photo to your Home or Lock screen, email, tweet or even print it (If you have a compatible wireless printer). The 'Assign to Contact' menu choice is also useful for adding images next to your contacts' names.

04 Remove red-eye
Edit an image containing people with red-eye and click the Red-Eye option. Next, click on the people's eyes to remove the red where necessary. Click Save to finish.

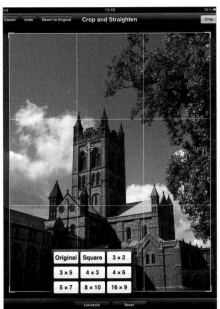

05 Crop photo
Edit an image and then click Crop. Drag a finger to resize the photo. You can click on Constrain to maintain the aspect ratio. Select Crop at the top, then Save.

06 Undo changes
If you have made a mistake, hit Undo at the top. Also, after an image has been edited you can choose 'Revert to Original' to return to the unedited photo.

Create a slideshow

 App used: Photos   **Time needed:** 15 minutes

Show your best pictures off with a cool slideshow, complete with transitions and your own music

Apple has taken a lot of time over the Photos app on the iPad. We know this because it's a completely different app to the one that appears on the iPhone, even though they both share the same operating system. One of the things that sets this new Photos app apart is its ability to show incredible picture slideshows, with far more control than the iPhone equivalent. A large part of this is, of course, down to the larger screen with greater resolution, but another part is the way the interface is so easy to use that you'll really enjoy creating and watching them with friends.

Once you've learned how to create a slideshow, we're confident that you'll be so impressed that you'll be making them all the time. The real shame is that, unlike the desktop version in iPhoto, you can't save the results and share them with others. For now, though, just enjoy the brilliance of these slideshows.

"iPad's Photos can show picture slideshows with far more control than the iPhone equivalent"

Photos Setting up a slideshow

01 Load it, tap it
Load the Photos app from your home screen and then navigate to an album or a picture that you like. Then tap the 'Slideshow' button at the top of the interface to begin.

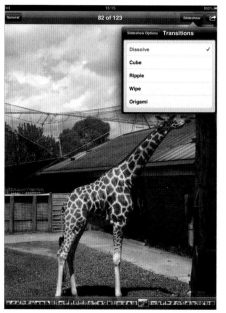

02 Options
The options window will now appear and you can begin to customise your slideshow. Tap on the transition you wish to use between photos. You have the choice of five different ones.

03 Tune it
You can add music to the slideshow by tapping the music button. This will bring up all of your songs that have been synced from iTunes, so if you want a specific song make sure it's on there.

The iPad slideshow interface

Be amazed at how simply you can create a beautiful slideshow

Transitions
Origami is a new Apple transition type and it basically looks as though photos are folding out from under each other. Very cool

Pop-ups
Having windows within windows makes navigation on the iPad a complete joy. You pretty much always stay on the same page

Rotation
As you would expect, the photos will auto-rotate when the iPad is itself rotated. This way you can get the most from both portrait and landscape pictures

Scrubber
The Photos app has a cool and very easy to use scrubber at the bottom of the interface, so you can navigate through a large number of pictures very easily

Sounds
The integration of music into the slideshow adds a whole new dimension to watching your pictures. Your music can really set the mood. It is possible to create a playlist from the Music app on the iPad, so you can create something specific on the fly.

04 Playlist it
If you are really organised you will have already created a custom playlist for the slideshow and can use this now. Tap on whatever you wish to use to select it and you're just about ready to go.

05 Ready, steady
Once you have everything in place, just tap the 'Start Slideshow' button at the bottom of the 'Slideshow Options' window. Your slideshow will begin immediately with your chosen settings.

06 Watch in awe
You can now relax with the iPad, watching your favourite pictures from your most recent holiday or event and listening to your favourite tunes while you do it. It's as simple as that.

Use Photo Stream to sync your photos

Take advantage of Apple's iCloud service to get your photos automatically pushed to all of your devices

One of the handiest new features of iOS 5 is Photo Stream. Using your own personal iCloud, with Photo Stream activated, you can get photos transported automatically – and totally wirelessly – to all of your iOS 5/Mac OS X 10.7.2 devices on the same Wi-Fi network. So if you take a picture on your iPhone, within seconds it will appear on your iPad. If you take some snaps on your iPad 2 then they will be beamed to your iPhone and your Mac without you having to lift a finger. The whole process eradicates the need to email individual images, or copy them onto portable storage devices to transport across to your other devices. It's a quick and convenient process that just occurs in the background.

In order to set up Photo Stream, you must first set up your iCloud account. This is a free service that replaces Apple's MobileMe service and it provides a host of great features, such as the option to sync documents and files, music, bookmarks, contact details and calendar events across all of your devices, as well as backing up your important data. Setting up iCloud is easy: you go to Settings, tap on the 'iCloud' section and then log in with your standard Apple ID (the same email address and password that you use for your other Apple services, such as the App Store and iTunes). In this tutorial we guide you through the process.

Photos How to activate your Photo Stream

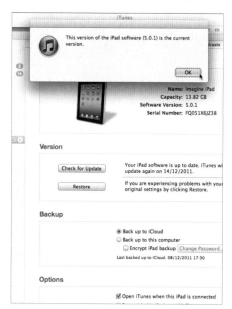

01 Update to iOS 5

Photo Stream is a service that comes as part of the iOS 5 operating system, so connect your device to your computer through iTunes and ensure that you have the latest free software update installed on your device.

02 Activate your iCloud

With iOS 5 installed, go to Settings>iCloud and then activate your free iCloud account by logging in with your Apple ID (the same email address and password that you use to log in to the other Apple services).

03 Turn on Photo Stream

You have full freedom of which iCloud services you use and you can toggle them on or off from Settings>iCloud. Included in the list of compatible apps is 'Photo Stream', so move the slider to 'On' to activate it.

Your synced photos

Thanks to Photo Stream you need never manually transfer your photos again

Easy sharing
Once your images are in your Photos app, you can then easily share them with others via email, tweeting, attaching them to an SMS text message and more

Photo Stream
Once activated, Photo Stream will automatically update your Photos app with all of the images captured on other devices, wirelessly. Impressive, huh?

Tap, pinch, expand
All images that are automatically imported into your Photo Stream album can be tapped on, expanded and pinched to shrink like normal through your Photos app

Your photos
Your Photo Stream album will be updated as and when new images are captured on other devices linked to your iCloud. Take pictures, sit back and watch the magic happen

All cameras supported
Photo Stream isn't restricted to iDevices. If you plug a non-Apple digital camera into your Mac (which is running Mac OS X 10.7.2 with iCloud enabled), all of the images on that camera will also be automatically whipped off and pushed straight to your Photo Stream too. Now that really is impressive.

04 Take pictures

To discover the magic of Photo Stream, follow the previous steps on your iPhone device and then start taking photos. Within a minute, open up the Photos app on your iPad and then tap on the new 'Photo Stream' tab.

05 Instant transferal

As if by magic, all of the photos that you have taken on your iPhone will start appearing in your Photo Stream album, completely doing away with the need to manually transfer images by email or actually copying them across.

06 View and edit

You now have complete access to all of the photos taken on all of your devices and can go about editing them and sharing them with others – it's a great, seamless system that will save you hours of time and effort in the long run.

App used:
Camera

Time needed:
10 minutes

Taking video on your iPad

You probably didn't buy your iPad to record video, but it's an ability that shouldn't be overlooked

The old truism that the best camera is the one you have with you applies as much to shooting video as it does to taking snapshots. You might be browsing the internet, reading a book or listening to music on your iPad 2, but within seconds you can use it to quickly grab priceless footage of that never-to-be-repeated moment.

In fact, the iPad 2 is equipped with two cameras: one front and one rear-facing. And while you'll probably get a lot of use out of the front-facing camera thanks to the FaceTime and Photo Booth apps, the better quality of the rear camera makes it more suitable for recording video.

While you can't really argue that the iPad allows the sort of unobtrusive video recording of its much smaller iPod touch or iPhone siblings – to be fair, using it to shoot video does feel a bit awkward the first time you do it – the tablet device's large screen makes it surprisingly easy to produce good results, particularly when it comes to focusing and exposure settings.

Once you've taken the footage, it's also simple to process and edit the results to send to friends or family. Here's how to get the best out of it.

Camera Shooting video with the iPad

01 Launch the video
Tap the Camera app's icon on your iPad's screen to launch it. Slide the Camera/Video slider (bottom right) toward the video camera icon to turn the video camera on.

02 Recording video
Tap the record button to begin recording. As you record, the red record button will slowly pulse, while at the top right of the screen the elapsed time is displayed.

03 Change focus or exposure
To change the focus of the video or set its exposure tap at the point where you want to set the focus or the exposure, and the rest of the video will adjust to compensate.

Recording video footage
How to control your camera

Front or back?
When you're not recording, an icon appears in the upper-right corner of the screen that lets you switch between the front and rear cameras

Controlling recordings
The record button pulses as you record and the viewfinder displays the elapsed recording time. Just tap the Record button to stop recording

Camera quality
You'll get better results with the rear-facing camera, which records HD video at up to 30 frames per second, than the lower-resolution front camera

Lock focus
You can lock the focus and exposure by simply tapping and holding in the viewfinder until the focus box pulses and shows 'AE Lock'

Get the light right
The secret to capturing good quality video on the iPad 2 is to make sure you use it in well-lit conditions. Both front and rear-facing cameras perform less well in low light conditions, so you'll get the best results if you record your video outside in the daytime or, if inside, where there is plenty of available light.

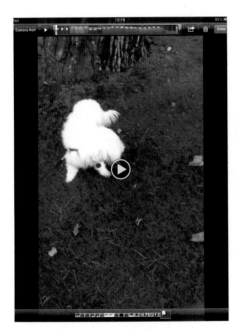

04 Stopping recording
Tap the record button again to turn recording off. A thumbnail link to your freshly created video appears at the bottom left of the screen. Tap it to view the video you've just taken.

05 Edit the video
You can trim this video by dragging the start and end points on the filmstrip at the top of the screen and dragging the yellow handles inwards. When you're happy, tap the Trim button.

06 Share with others
To share your completed video with others, tap the arrow icon to the top right of the screen and select the appropriate option from the drop-down menu that appears.

App used: Photo Booth

 Time needed: 5 minutes

Take photos with Photo Booth

Photo Booth is capable of applying weird and wonderful camera effects and using both the front and rear-facing cameras on your iPad 2. It's a bit crazy, but also tremendous fun…

 Photo Booth made its debut on the Mac some years ago, when built-in iSight cameras became standard across most models of Apple computers. Now thanks to the cameras on the iPad 2, it has made its way to the device and it's a fun way to take snapshots of yourself and your friends, or just to take strange-looking photos of anything you can point a camera at.

The app itself is a little more limited on the iPad for some reason, with fewer effects and without the ability to record video with effects, but it's still great fun to play with. The touch screen interface means that when effects have a focus point, which is to say that they distort the image based on a certain area of the screen, you can use your finger to change the position and so edit the effect. Some of the others are just on or off – they can't be edited. Of course you are also able to use either the front or rear-facing cameras depending on whether you wish to photograph yourself or someone else.

"It's certainly a fun way to take snapshots of yourself and your friends"

Photo Booth Take pictures in Photo Booth

01 Fire it up

Open Photo Booth and it should default to using the front-facing camera. You'll see a range of different crazy effects and if you tap on one, you will get to see that effect in full screen.

02 Light Tunnel

This is the Light Tunnel effect and if you drag with your finger, you will be able to position the centre of the effect over any part of the screen. This applies to other effects that distort the image.

Using Photo Booth

Use Photo Booth's wacky effects to create fun and outlandish pictures to share or use on social networking sites…

Take a picture
Press the shutter button to take a snapshot and the image will be saved to a special camera roll inside Photo Booth. Form there, pictures can be deleted, viewed or emailed

The image
The weird and wonderful results of Photo Booth's effects can be seen on the main screen. This is a thermographic effect

Camera flip
The iPad 2 has both front and rear-facing cameras and you can flip between them by using this icon. The effects all work the same way through both of the cameras

Effects
To return to the effects list, click the effects icon. You will be able to choose from the built-in effects such as pinch, twirl, X-ray, mirror and a host of other strange ones

Hardware requirements
The kinds of real-time image processing performed by Photo Booth actually place quite a strain on hardware, though the reason it isn't included on the iPad 1 is because it doesn't have any cameras. You're not able at present to apply Photo Booth effects to video on the iPad, though this may be something that Apple chooses to unlock with a software update at some point in the future.

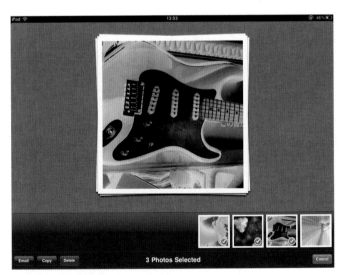

03 View your pictures

Pictures that you take are shown along the bottom. Scroll around and load up any one to view it full screen. Click the camera chooser to flip to the rear camera, or the effect icon to choose a different effect.

04 Share pictures

Click on the Share button and you can choose a number of pictures to either place in an email, copy, or delete. They are shown in a helpful stack view. If you deselect a picture it 'slides' out of the stack.

 App used:
Videos

 Time needed:
10 minutes

Get the most out of iPad videos

The iPad is perfectly designed for the mobile movie experience thanks to its large screen

 The Videos feature alone has the potential to keep you occupied on long plane journeys, in hotels or waiting rooms, and adds a use to the iPad that could justify half of the cost straight away. It has been designed for ease of use, as most Apple software is, and takes care of many of the niggles found in competing devices. For example, it will automatically play a film from the point you left it, and expanding the screen requires a simple double tap.

Everything is designed to help you get the most from the experience, but some tips are still useful to get you off to a flying start. In this step-by-step we will show you how to obtain new movies, how to transfer them to your iPad and how to make the most of the viewing experience. You could easily do all of this yourself, but in this instance a little knowledge certainly goes a long way and missing out on the movie capabilities of the iPad would be a real shame given the benefits it offers.

"The Video feature alone adds a use to the iPad that could justify half of the cost straight away"

Videos Make the most of movies

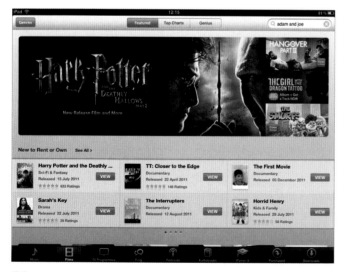

01 Grab a film

The easiest way to obtain good quality content is via iTunes. Navigate to the Films or TV Programmes section and choose the film you would like to rent or buy. You can also try some free trailers to get started without spending any money.

02 Put it on the iPad

Your purchases will be downloaded and stored on your iPad. If you have iCloud activated then they will also automatically be pushed to your other devices, such as your Mac or iPhone wirelessly, allowing you to view them on those devices too.

Watch movies on your iPad

Get the most out of the Videos app

Full screen
Tapping on this icon will alternate between full-screen and widescreen viewing. You can also double tap anywhere on screen to achieve this effect

Full control
You can move to specific parts of a video by moving the slider at the top with your finger; the further down the screen your finger is, the more precise the movement

Back where you left off
Videos automatically remembers where you finished watching and will start any film at that exact place when you open it up again

Main controls
The main control keys are standard and are brought up by tapping the screen once. You can play, pause, forward or rewind when you need to

HD
Many iTunes movies and TV programmes are now offered in HD format, which offers a much crisper viewing experience. Sometimes you will pay more for the video, but think of it in a similar way to paying more for Blu-ray. These files will also be larger in size, sometimes significantly, so make sure you have adequate space before you buy.

03 The fun starts here

All you need to do now is simply click the Videos icon and choose the film you want to watch from the list of videos that you have installed on your iPad. The film (or TV programme, for that matter) will immediately start to play from the beginning.

04 Small changes

Double-tapping the screen will make the movie play in full-screen mode, and doing so again will take it back to standard format (which is useful for widescreen films). The rest of the on-screen tweaks are obvious in their implementation, such as play, pause, etc.

App used:
YouTube

Time needed:
10 minutes

Access video content via YouTube

Discover how to get the most out of YouTube on your iPad

The built-in YouTube iPad app is a lesson in thoughtful design, and manages to bring the desktop experience to a mobile device while maintaining all of the functionality of the main web portal YouTube uses. With a YouTube account in place you can save favourites, share videos with friends and comment on videos you like, and your changes will be accessible on your desktop automatically. It all sounds very simple and on the whole it is, but some pointers will help you to get even more out of the experience.

It is worth remembering that, should you use the service on a 3G iPad, you will be pushing a hefty amount of data so be aware of the limits your network provider has imposed on your account. Wi-Fi is the recommended solution for YouTube-use on an iPad because it speeds up the loading of videos and also makes the experience feel more like the one you have come to expect on a desktop. The iPad YouTube app really does bring every feature to your mobile life, and here we will show you how to get up and running in no time and how to make the most of its potential. It's all free so you have no reason not to try it for yourself.

YouTube   Make the most of YouTube

01 Getting started

To utilise every feature in YouTube for the iPad you will need an account. Go to **www.youtube. com** and click the Create Account option in the top right-hand corner.

02 Create an account

Complete the requested information and then set up a new Google account (or use your current account in the next page). This completes the process for setting up a new YouTube account.

03 Make YouTube personal

On the iPad, open the YouTube app and tap Favourites, then tap the Sign In icon, and input your username and password. You will now have access to your videos, favourites and more.

YouTube on iPad

Once you discover how to use YouTube on your iPad, you may decide to use it as a replacement for the desktop version…

Search everything
You can search almost the entire YouTube database from your iPad in the same way you use a standard web search engine by typing in this box

Popular videos
The most recent popular videos of all time, from the past week and from today are a useful way to simply browse and see what's happening on YouTube

Keep it personal
Your main account information is kept up to date and is easily accessible via the handy icons at the bottom of each section

Previews
Each video is previewed with an icon, rating and the number of views, which together should tell you if it's worth watching

Streaming
Streaming video wirelessly is very bandwidth-hungry, and overuse on 3G alone could cause you to break the limit on your data account. Your network provider is then within its rights to send you a warning. When possible, try to use Wi-Fi because this will not only perform better, but could potentially save you a lot of money.

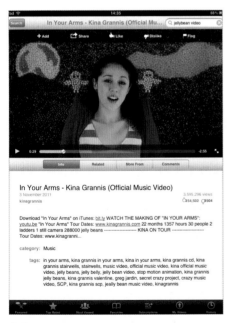

04 Explore the content
You can now explore the content within YouTube. When you tap a video to watch it you will see a selection of icons at the top of the screen that you can use to mark favourites or share videos.

05 Fully in step
Any changes that you make to your YouTube account on the iPad will be mirrored on your desktop, and vice versa, so you can use both and keep the changes intact.

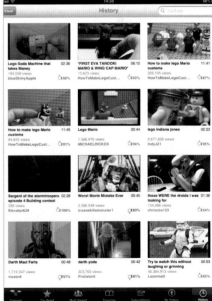

06 Keep track
YouTube includes a history icon (found along the bottom of the screen) that shows your most recently viewed videos. This is useful if you forget to add a viewed video to your favourites list.

App used:
Game Center

Time needed:
10 minutes

Set up a Game Center account

Enter into a world of fun games, fierce competition and social gaming with Game Center

Like Open Feint before it, Apple's Game Center is a multi-purpose gaming service that gives users a platform to befriend other gamers, engage in multiplayer, compete for online leaderboard supremacy and earn unlockable achievements. It comes preloaded on devices with iOS 4 and above installed, and it significantly enhances your iPad as a gaming platform.

Once you follow the initial set-up instructions, there is a wealth of options available to you. From the top menu you can clearly see your friend, game and achievement counters displayed, while the bottom tab bar lets you access Game Center's menus. 'Games' is by far the most in-depth, displaying all of your Game Center-enabled games, as well as your global ranking on the online leaderboards, something many people can become obsessed with.

Within each game's menu, you can also see how many achievements you have unlocked, get details on locked achievements and recommend the app to a friend. It's a solid service that brings together the best games available on one dedicated platform.

"It significantly enhances your iPad as a gaming platform"

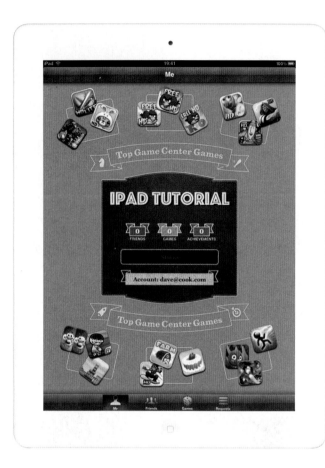

Game Center Set up your new account

01 Get updated

Game Center runs on iPads running iOS 4 and above. It's unlikely your device will be running anything less, but it always pays to ensure your iPad is running the latest firmware available. Hook it up to iTunes and download any new updates before proceeding.

02 Open an account

Once in Game Center, tap the 'Create New Account' option. The app will ask you to input your location and date of birth, as well as accepting the terms and conditions. This is straightforward, but the next step requires a bit of thought.

Welcome to Game Center

Enter a world of fun and friends

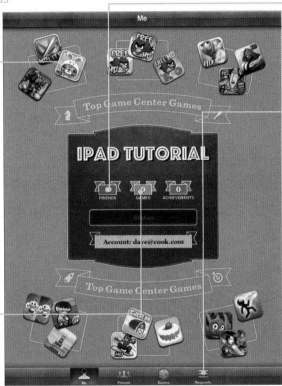

Your Friends list
Tapping 'Friends' will bring up a list of your connected friends, together with their achievements and recent games. In order for them to appear here, you must accept their friend request

Requests list
The 'Requests' tab houses your pending friends requests. You can also send out requests if you know the email address tethered to a person's Apple ID. Once a request is accepted, the person is instantly added to your list

Top Game Center games
Promoted or top-selling apps will refresh along the top and bottom of Game Center's top menu. You can tap app icons to be taken to their respective iTunes pages to buy them

The Games tab
Tapping 'Games' will bring up an overview of all your Games Center-enabled apps. Here, you can view achievements, online leaderboard rank, and recommend the app to friends

Rival platforms
Just like the console gaming world, iTunes plays host to two competing game platforms – Open Feint and Game Center – both vying for a place as the best gaming format the iOS has to offer. Both services have a wealth of superb features, such as Game Center's social features and Open Feint's free game deals. Both are well worth trying.

03 Register with iTunes
On the next page, you will be asked to input more data. Entering the email address associated with your existing Apple ID will automatically add your Game Center-enabled apps to the library. Otherwise, enter an unassociated email address to start from scratch.

04 Start playing today
Once your details have been entered, the app will return to the top menu. In the 'Games' tab you can get your account started properly by tapping 'Find Game Center Games'. This will take you straight to iTunes so you can start building your library.

Get more out of Game Center

Explore your iOS gaming hub and discover how to get games, find friends and beat your mates online

 PSN, Xbox Live... all the best games consoles have their own online channel for you to find friends, chat and engage in some multiplayer action – and your iPad is no different. Game Center is your iOS gaming hub and through it you can set up a gaming profile, discover the latest games and play against friends.

Finding your way around Game Center is easy and, once your profile has been set up, you can submit high scores for the online leaderboards and get achievements that contribute to your overall Game Center score. Finding new games is simple, as you can get recommendations and search what you are looking for, all from within your Game Center app, which means you only install games that are compatible with the service. You can still install games by browsing through the App Store, but be sure to look out for the Game Center logo to ensure they're compatible. When you have compiled a friends list, you can then compare scores and play against each other.

"You can submit your high scores for the online leaderboards"

Game Center Finding friends and getting games

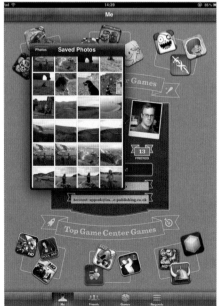

01 Setting your status

Adding a status to your Game Center allows you to apply some personality to your profile. Tap the text box in the middle of the screen and then enter a message of intent.

02 Adding a photo

You can assign a photo to your profile by either tapping on the photo frame or selecting the 'Change Photo' option. Choose an image from your Camera Roll to assign.

03 Finding friends

To add new friends, tap the Friends icon to view your current friends list and then tap the '+' icon in the top-left corner. Then enter an email address or nickname (if you know it).

Your personal Game Center

Finding your way around your gaming hub

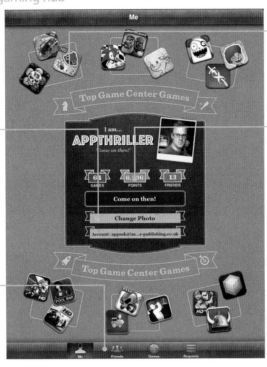

Recommended games
The app icons surrounding your profile are game recommendations. Tap on an icon to be taken to the App Store to learn more and purchase it

Your profile
Your nickname, status and photo will be proudly displayed on the main 'Me' page of your Game Center app. Tap the photo and text box to change them

Your Game Center score
Achievements you earn in compatible games are calculated into scores which are added to your running total. This is your overall Game Center score to compare and complete with those of your friends

Game Center sections
You can easily jump to your friends list, the games currently on your device (and thousands that aren't) and find friends via the tabs located at the bottom of the screen

Online gaming
All of your iPad gaming is channelled through Game Center, including the ability to play against your friends online. Ensure that both you and your friend have the same game installed on your device and then select the multiplayer options in-game. You will now be able to connect to your friend through Game Center and give them a sound thrashing.

04 Get games
Tap on the Games tab and you can view all the Game Center-compatible games on your device. You can get more games by tapping the Game Recommendations option at the top of the page.

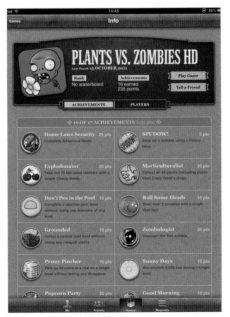

05 Earn achievements
You earn achievements and Game Center points by completing certain feats within games. To view a game's available achievements, tap Games and then choose a game and tap Achievements.

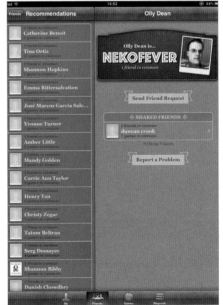

06 Friend recommendations
New to iOS 5 is a feature that recommends new friends based on the games you play and existing friends. In the Friends tab, tap Recommendations in the top-left corner.

App used:
Music

Time needed:
10 minutes

Get to know the new Music app in iOS 5

We guide you around your iPad's new-look iPod app and show you how to make a playlist

Your iPad's Music app (previously the iPod app) is your mobile music player and superstore all rolled into one. With a clean, simple, easy to manipulate interface that is great fun to play with, you can play any tracks stored in your library by tapping on it and using the payback controls, create your own Playlists on the fly and even visit the iTunes Store from within the app to buying something new. What's more, if you have enabled your iCloud (the free cloud storage and syncing service that comes free with iOS 5), any new music you purchase will be pushed to all of your iOS 5 devices without you having to lift a finger. By the same process you can also access and download music that you have downloaded in the past at no extra cost.

In this tutorial we guide you through the intricacies of this versatile app and show you how to create Playlists, access your purchased music files and much more.

Music Create a playlist

01 Launch the app

If you have recently updated to iOS 5 then you may be wondering where your iPod app has disappeared to. It has been replaced by the Music app, which can be found in your Dock by default.

02 Browse songs

Use the tiles at the bottom of the screen to browse your music by Playlist, Songs, Artists or Albums. Tap on a song to start playing it. The playback controls are at the top of the screen.

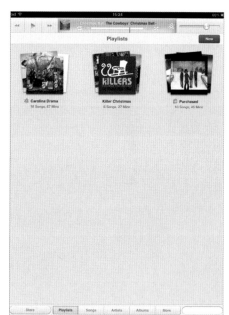

03 Make a Playlist

Tap on the Playlist tile and then tap 'New' in the top-right corner. Give your new Playlist a name, then add songs from your library, drag them into a preferred order and then tap 'Done'.

Music while you're mobile

Setting up playlists on the iPad is a breeze

Playback controls
The playback controls, including play/pause, fast forward and rewind, are situated across the top of the Music app window, along with the volume slider and details about the song that is currently playing

Full control
You can move to specific parts of a song by moving the slider at the top with your finger

Library tabs
The tiles at the bottom of the screen let you browse your music library in whatever way you wish. There is also a handy search window to the right

More music
You can purchase and download additional music at any time by tapping on the 'Store' button. This will take you to what is essentially the iTunes app, but it saves a little time

iTunes in the Cloud
You can still add converted CD tracks on your Mac to your iPad by connecting then two and dragging them across, but with iCloud enabled you can get any new purchased music pushed to all of your devices, including your Mac and your iPhone.

04 Visit the iTunes Store
You can make new purchases from within the Music app by tapping the 'Store' button. You can then browse the full iTunes Store and download new tracks, albums and podcasts.

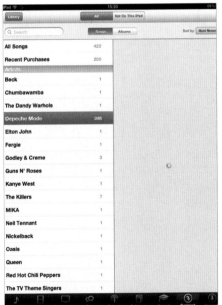

05 Connect to iCloud
Through iCloud you can get all of your previous iTunes purchases beamed directly to your iPad. Create an account and connect, then go to the 'Purchased' category in the iTunes Store.

06 Get familiar with the settings
Go to 'Settings' and then tap 'Music' to access the app's preferences. Here you can set the EQ to the style of music you are playing, set a cap on how high the volume goes and more.

The next step

 App used:
iTunes

 Time needed:
5 minutes

Create Genius playlists on the iPad

Making your own special playlist is great but by letting the iPad do
all the hard work you can get some really cool musical mixes

Keeping track of all the music on your iPad can be a bit
of a pain. It's surprising how much music you can fit
onto even just the 16GB version. With all that music it
makes sense to keep track of it all and to create playlists.

Of course, listening to whole albums is fine, but then we all have
our favourite tracks and like to hear them more often than others.
Creating playlists manually is a great way of doing this, but it's time
consuming and if you don't keep them updated they soon get
tiresome.

You could just stick your whole music collection on random, but
even this throws up issues like those hidden tracks or fillers that
ruin a smooth transition, or the odd song you're bored of hearing.
The best solution may well be Genius mixes.

Apple has created a tool that lets you select a track and
automatically create a playlist of music that complements each
other. It's a great way of keeping the music going around a certain
theme and in the main it's incredibly reliable.

"We all have our favourite
tracks and like to hear them
more often than others"

Music Make Genius mixes on the iPad

01 Open Music

Fire up your iPad and then launch the new-look Music application. Your
music can be displayed in a number of ways using the tabs along the
bottom. Scroll until you find a song that would make a good foundation for
your playlist; this will be the basis of your list.

02 Make a Genius mix

When you have found a track that most suits your current mood, tap
on it to start it playing. When you're ready, tap on the Genius symbol that
you can find across the top bar next to the running time and the name, artist
and album name.

The Genius interface

Where to go to control your playlist

Controls
The iOS 5 update provided a complete new look for music on your iPad, and the basic controls can now be found up here in the top-left corner

Views
To view your music collection in a number of different views simply tap on one of the options. Making Genius mixes is simpler if you view your music as Songs, however

Save your playlist
By clicking the Save button you will store your new Genius playlist in the Music application on your iPad

Refresh
Clicking Refresh will update the tracks that make up your playlist

Genius mixes
Contrary to what you might think, Genius mixes aren't just randomly thrown together and Apple is working behind the scenes to make the music fit. iTunes assesses your music collection and from an extensive database puts together the tracks that go best.

03 Asses your mix

You'll see that a new playlist called Genius Playlist has been added to your library. It will be populated by the single track that you just selected. From this screen you can also create a new playlist if you're ready to move on.

04 Save your playlist

By clicking on your Genius playlist, it will display all the songs that have been compiled for you. From here you can save the playlist, or click Refresh if you want to add any more songs to the mix. Your playlist will now be up and running.

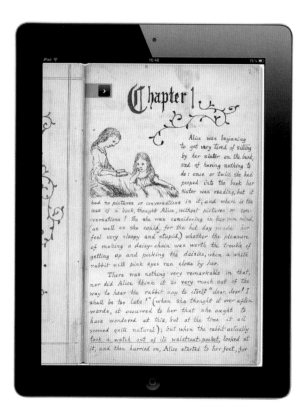

App used:
iBooks

Time needed:
10 minutes

Purchase an iBook

Learn how to buy an iBook and open up to a whole world of digital reading

One of the reasons for the iPad's existence is to take on Amazon's Kindle. It's very easy to get lost in a world of crazy apps, accelerometers and multi-touch gestures, but the iPad was conceived to be a fantastic eBook reader. It obviously has a number of advantages over the Kindle in that it can do a great deal more than a dedicated device, but on a purely eBook-reading scale, the iPad is still one of the most advanced out there. What's more is that Apple already has a tried and tested way to deliver eBooks directly to its device: namely the iTunes Store. Apple hasn't just bundled the new books into that system, though, because it's created a separate space for these so that users can be sure of what they are downloading.

Once you've downloaded the app, iBooks holds all your eBooks, and from there you can access the custom-built iBooks Store to make purchases, which get downloaded directly. The system is magnificently simple and makes impulse buys a regular occurrence. This tutorial will take you through your first download from iBooks so you can get a feel for the system. It's then up to you to resist buying a library's worth of content on each visit!

> **"The iBooks system is magnificently simple and makes impulse buys a regular occurrence"**

iBooks Purchase a book

01 Load and launch
You have to download iBooks from the App Store and then, once it's loaded, have a look at the free copy of Winnie The Pooh. To purchase your first book, hit the Store button on the top left.

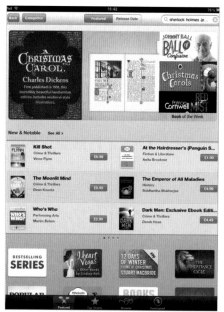

02 Familiar feel
The iBooks Store is very much like the App Store or the iTunes Store. Books are categorised and searchable, and everything is charted so that you can see what is selling best.

03 Top charts
The 'Featured' section displays all of the latest releases of significance and you can also tap on 'Top Charts' at the bottom of the screen to see which titles are currently popular.

The iBooks Store homepage

Find your way around your new home for digital books

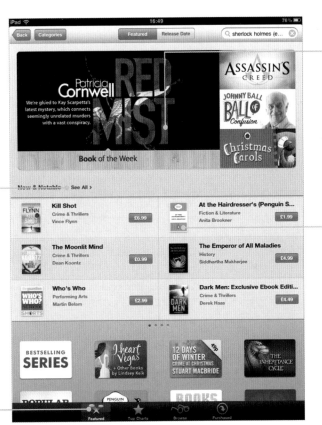

Promo perfection
Again, like the App Store, books are picked by Apple to be featured on the front of the Store. This positioning increases their sales no end, as you can imagine

See All
Use the See All button in order to get a bigger list from any given section. It's the same system that's used on the App Store

Easy nav
Navigating through the Store with your fingers is easy. Tap buttons to see more and tap individual books in order to get more information

Tabs at the bottom
At the bottom of the interface there are four tabs, which will help you navigate through the Store and also see what you have already bought

iCloud
You can sync your book collection and bookmarks to iCloud, so that they will be available across all of your iOS 5 devices. Go to Settings> iBooks to activate and take advantage of these services.

04 Free classics
Like the App Store, there are a huge number of free books. These tend to be the classics, so you can go ahead and get great content for nothing. Tap on the Free button and then tap Get Book.

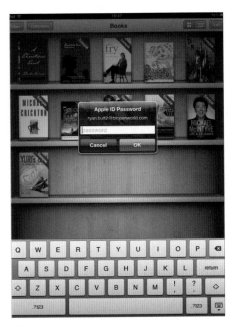

05 Password
You'll now be returned to the bookshelf and prompted to enter your iTunes account password. Do so and, once done, tap the OK button to begin the download.

06 New books
Your new books will now appear on the bookshelf and you'll see a progress bar as they download. Once downloaded, the book will become available to read at your leisure.

Getting to know iBooks

 App used:
iBooks

 Time needed:
10 minutes

Having an eBook reader on the iPad is very cool, so here's how to customise it to your liking…

Despite the conjecture, if you've actually used the iPad you'll know full well that it's much more than just a large iPod touch. The size really does make it feel like you're holding a full-blown computer in your hands, and no other app exemplifies the difference more than iBooks. When you're reading a book on the iPad it feels natural, it's easy to do, and we are certain that we'll be doing a lot more reading now that it's so simple to carry books around with us. The beauty of the iPad interface means that making changes to the way iBooks looks is very, very simple. Users can opt to make text bigger, change the font and alter the brightness of the book without having to leave the page they are reading. Try doing the same three operations on an iPhone and see how many times you have to leave and return to the page you are reading. iBooks is exceptional, so follow our quick tutorial on how to get more from the already excellent reading experience.

True text
With the iPad being the size it is, reading is a complete joy. Once you have your fonts and the brightness set up how you like, you can read for hours on this device

Scrubber
You can also navigate through the app using the scrubber bar at the bottom of the page. Just drag your finger along the line

"Users can make text bigger, change the font and alter the brightness of the book"

iBooks Font, size and brightness

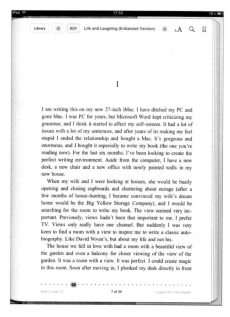

01 Open, bask
Open the iBooks app and then tap on the cover of a book on your shelf that you would like to read. The page is presented as if it were a real book but with options at the top and bottom.

02 Contents
You can navigate from the contents page to a chapter by tapping on it, and once you've been reading a while, you can head straight to your own bookmarks within the pages themselves.

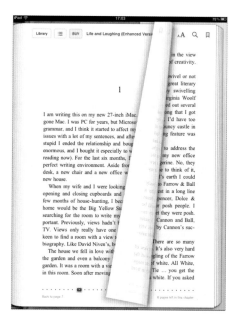

03 Curler
You can flip through pages by dragging from the right-hand side to the left, where you'll see the cool page curl. Or you can use the less cool but more functional tap on the right-hand side.

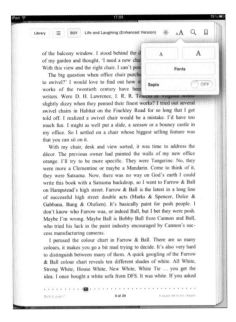

04 Font it

Tap on the 'aA' font button at the top to access the menu where you can alter the book's font and text size. Tap the big A to increase font size and the small one to decrease it.

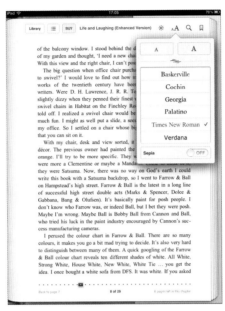

05 Font type

To change the font type, tap the Fonts button and then pick from the available options that are listed in the pop-out window. The selection should provide an alternative that suits you.

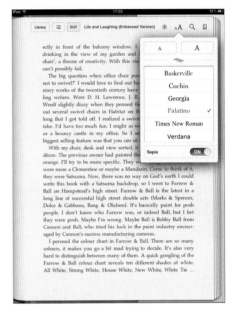

06 Tick it, watch it

Tap the font you wish to select and a tick will appear next to it. As with all the other changes you can make to the appearance of a book within iBooks, they happen instantly.

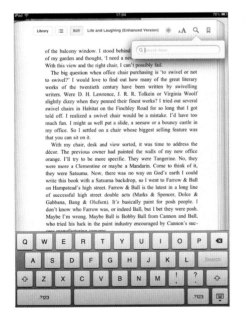

07 Spotlight index

Tap on the magnifying glass icon to bring up a search field. Every book on the iBook Store is fully indexed so you can instantly find individual words in a book – invaluable for textbooks.

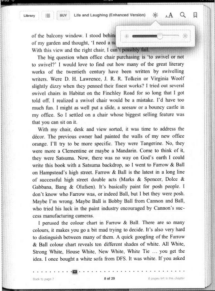

08 Brightness

Tap on the sunshine icon to bring up brightness settings of the book. This only affects the levels within iBooks and doesn't translate to the rest of the iPad, so you won't have to change it back.

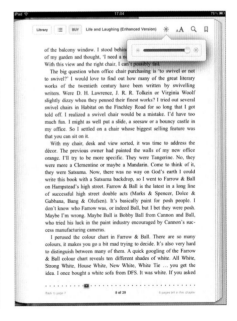

09 Suitable setting

Changing the brightness means that you can alter the reading light to whatever is most comfortable for your eyes. The brighter the ambient light, the brighter iBooks needs to be.

 App used:
Newsstand

 Time needed:
20 minutes

Set up a subscription on Newsstand

The built-in app allows you to subscribe to your favourite magazines and get the new issue on release day

One of the great new features of iOS 5 is the Newsstand app, which lets you keep on top of all your favourite reading with ease. This built-in app enables you to create your own personal magazine library, and has its own dedicated store for you to purchase and download from. The excitement for Newsstand stems from the fact that it means new developers have started afresh on their tablet publications, learning from previous mistakes to provide a better reading experience this time around for iOS 5 users. The other big positive with Newsstand is that you can set up subscriptions to your favourite magazines, so you never miss an issue, and have each one download to your Newsstand library and be accessible to you anywhere.

More and more magazines are becoming available via Newsstand and the App Store, so the amount of choice is growing constantly, each publication trying to stand out from the crowd with interactive features and extra content. Setting up a subscription is a simple process and a good way to get your bearings should you be new to iOS.

"This built-in app enables you to create your own personal magazine library"

Newsstand Purchase a subscription

01 Open Newsstand
On your Home screen, tap the Newsstand icon to open up the app and see your current library of magazine titles on the shelves. This is where all your downloaded items are displayed.

02 Visit the Store
To start your magazine search, tap the Store button at the top right of the Newsstand display. This will take you to the dedicated Newsstand wing of the App Store.

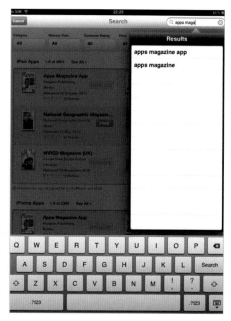

03 Search the Store
Here you can browse through all the magazines on sale – either using the various breakdowns provided by the Store, or by tapping Featured or Release Date and then using the search bar.

Making sense of the Newsstand Store

Find your way around this magazine archive

Search

If you click Featured or Release Date, it will bring up a search box so you can do a more direct search of the App Store

Featured titles

At the top of this page is the animated Featured window, where a selection of the most popular titles are displayed and so this is a good place to start your browsing

Info

When you find a magazine for you, don't just tap Install; instead tap the icon and get the extra info, including reviews and cost of each issue

Menu tabs

Along the bottom of the screen you have various tabs to help you navigate, including charts of the bestselling apps as well as Genius, which offers you download suggestions

Auto Subscriptions

Always keep track of your subscriptions as some automatically renew without you physically tapping to do so. Make a note if a title you download tells you this, which it will do, so you don't get a nasty surprise when you get your bank statement six months after you thought a subscription had ended.

04 Install and download

Once you've found the title you were after, tap Install and enter your iTunes password to download it to your Newsstand library, where you can access back issues and set up subscriptions.

05 What's on offer

It may take a few minutes for the title to download, but once it has, tap the cover to enter its personal library, and tap the Subscribe icon to see what options are on offer before purchasing.

06 Start reading

Once you've chosen your subscription and entered your password, the latest issue will become available in the magazine's library. Tap it to download, and start reading.

The next step

App used:
Pages

Time needed:
10 minutes

Get to grips with Pages

Apple's Pages takes the mobile word-processing experience to a whole new level

 Pages is not like most word processors – it combines the most used features in an interface which includes very few icons. Getting to know the app is not difficult, although it does help to understand where the main functions reside in order to get you started, and doing so will open up the power within. Despite the rather sparse interface, it is packed with formatting options and clever little tricks that make previously tiresome manoeuvres a thing of the past. For example, you can move an embedded image around an article and the words will automatically reposition themselves around it, and the included templates are completely customisable, which enables you to get creating in no time at all.

Not all specific needs are catered for, such as a word count, but Apple has done a good job of defining the most used functions that people need and being able to share your creations without touching a desktop is another advantage. You can even decide which format to save these documents in and, best of all, if you have iCloud enabled then you can sync your pages wirelessly between devices – so you can start a new layout on your iPad and finish it later on your iPhone or Mac. In this tutorial we guide you through the basics of this incredible versatile app.

Pages Create stunning documents on the move

01 Grab the app
Search for 'Pages' in iTunes and purchase and install as normal. £5.99 may seem expensive for an iTunes app, but it is in fact very good value for a word processor with so many features.

02 Have a look around
Pages is so obviously visual in the way it is designed that you could just have a wander around the icons and start typing, but the best place to start is the pre-loaded user manual.

03 Create your first document
In the first screen tap the '+' icon at the top and then tap New document. This will bring up a screen with templates on. You can choose anything from a blank page to a party invitation.

Making the most of Pages

Learn all the tricks of the Pages trade...

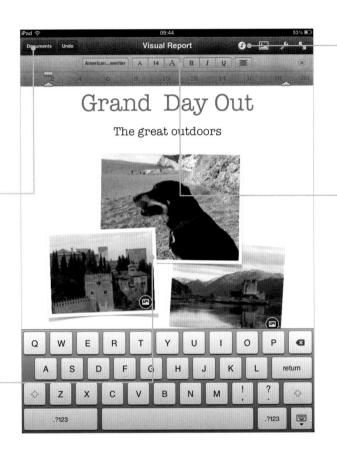

Extra formatting
Simply tap the 'i' icon to access extra formatting features such as bullet points, subtitles and headings. The options automatically change if you have an image highlighted

Document handling
Your completed documents are never far away. A tap of the 'My Documents' icon will bring up a page showing all of your saved work. Each document is saved automatically after every change

All the standards
All of the standard formatting options such as bold, italics and underline are easily accessible from the top bar. Highlight a word and click an icon for the desired effect

Easy image manipulation
Once inserted, images can be resized, moved and even twisted to the position you need. The words will automatically move to around them and into the right position

Work with templates
Templates can make the process of creating eye-catching documents incredibly easy and Pages includes a variety of styles. Once you create a new document using a template you can change the images and all of the background text to your needs. You can also create your own templates for future use.

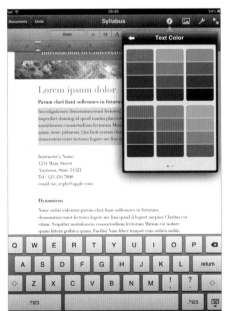

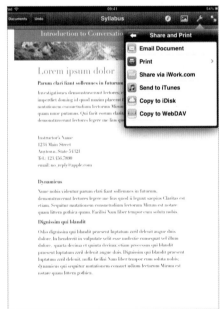

04 Test the options
Type a few words and then check the formatting options at the top. Select words by tapping and holding, at which point you can use the icons to format the text. Clicking 'i' gives further options.

05 Delve deeper
Other options include a document setup wizard, defined by the top-right spanner icon and a quick tap of the picture icon lets you insert an image into your document.

06 Share your work
You never need to save your work because Pages does it whenever a change is made, but you can export it to PDF, Pages or Word format and send by email with the tap of one icon.

Create spreadsheets with Numbers

Use Numbers to create serious or silly spreadsheets to suit all tastes

App used: Numbers

Time needed: 10 minutes

Spreadsheets are a part of everyone's lives these days and have taken on multiple roles in business and at home. Most spreadsheet programs tend to focus on the business side because this is where they are mainly used, but spreadsheets have a myriad of other uses that aren't often explored.

Numbers puts multiple uses front and centre with special templates built in and also brings a new way of working to the mobile user. However, the interface and function locations may feel alien to those that have used Excel for a long time and so a short introduction will help you to get to grips with the app quickly. There are a lot of functions built in to Numbers and some of these are not obvious, so take a look at these simple steps to start number-crunching straight away.

> "Mainly used in business, spreadsheets have many other uses that aren't often explored"

Tabs, tabs, tabs
You can create as many linked tabs as you like by simply tapping the '+' icon. When you need to view them, just move your finger from left to right until you find the one that you need

Touchy feely
You can adjust and select single cells, rows and columns with your finger and even though it feels strange at first, you will soon wonder how you ever created spreadsheets with just a mouse

Four icons
These four small icons are the shop window to a huge array of advanced functions including specialised calculations and standard formats

Numbers
Explore the power of this spreadsheet app

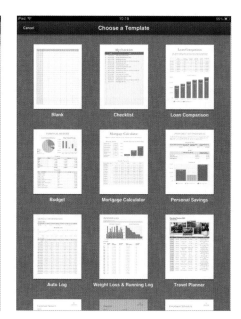

01 Grab the app
Numbers is available from the App Store. It costs £6.99, and although this may seem steep, it is excellent value even if you only need spreadsheets occasionally.

02 Check out the manual
Apple has included a manual in Numbers which highlights the various solutions it can be used for. Because of the large number of features on offer, it is recommended that you read it all.

03 Your first spreadsheet
Tap the '+' icon at the top and click the New Spreadsheet option. You'll now be offered a choice of templates which includes everything from a blank sheet to a mortgage calculator.

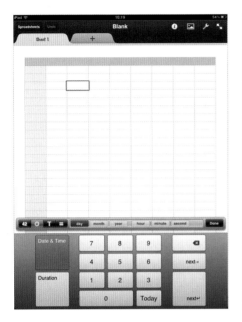

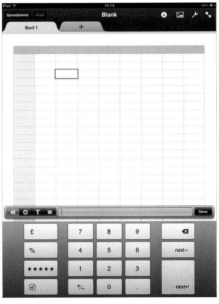

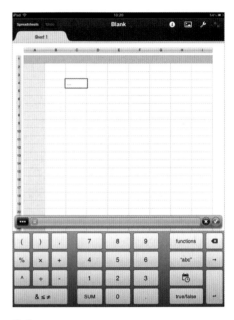

04 Add data

Choose the blank template option in the top-left corner and double-tap an empty cell. This brings up a dialog with four icons for numbers, date/time, text and formulas.

05 Handy shortcuts

Tapping any of the icons brings up a dialog with shortcuts pertinent to the data you want to input. For example the number icon will bring up a number pad plus a percentage button and more.

06 Use the data

Once you've understood where each function resides you can now do something with your content. Tap the '=' icon and you can choose from a wide range of simple functions that will pop up.

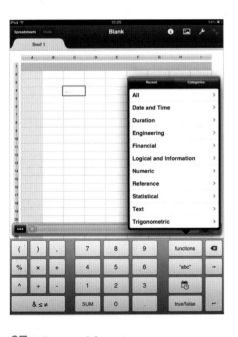

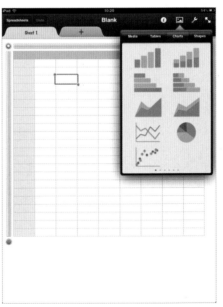

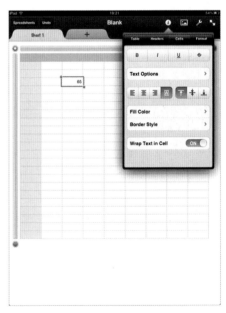

07 Advanced functions

The functions button is a window to some serious capability and includes categories of advanced functions such as Trigonometric, Engineering and Statistical.

08 Add some media

Once you have your basic data built you can tap the picture icon in the top-right and insert photos, tables and shapes which will help to make the data more visual.

09 Practise your touch

Numbers is touch only and this will present problems at first, but the more you practise the more natural it begins to feel. The interface looks simple, but it hides a huge range of options.

App used:
Keynote

Time needed:
10 minutes

Perform your presentations in style with Keynote

Keynote for iPad brings the Apple ethos of keeping things simple to the world of presentations

CHESS – A Whole New 'Take'

The classic hit musical gets re-imagined for 2012. If you think that you *know it so well*, prepare to be blown away! Oh Yeah!

Creating presentations in PowerPoint has caused as much scratching of heads over the years as almost any other software solution. Despite this, it has been widely used in the corporate world and still dominates the presentation software market. Keynote for iPad brings the advantages of being mobile and incredibly easy to use.

Because the iPad is finger driven, Apple has had to do away with the preciseness this type of software normally requires and has managed to make the entire process finger-friendly and much quicker than the competition. It will still take some time to get used to, though, because the commands are different and at times it feels almost too easy. In this guide we will show you how to create your first presentation and how to make the most of the features and the fact that you can create wherever you are without the need for wires.

> "Apple has managed to make the entire presentation process finger-friendly and much quicker"

Using Keynote

Make your presentations look professional without needing to touch your desktop PC or Mac

Use the icons
These four simple icons hold within them a wealth of tweaks and tricks that will help you build a presentation in no time at all

Check your slides
All of your slides are available in the left-hand column and are previewed in great detail. You can also drag and drop them to change the order in which they will appear

New slides
Adding a new slide requires a single tap on the '+' icon. Almost every function in Keynote only requires a tap or two and is highly intuitive to use

Shapes, text and more
The media available is almost unlimited and everything from simple text to photos and charts are available to you. You can then manipulate them once inserted into a slide

Keynote Build a Keynote presentation

01 Get Keynote

Keynote is available on the iTunes App Store for £5.99 and is part of the iWork for iPad solution. All you need to do is purchase it and install it on your iPad as normal.

02 Read the manual

As you would expect from Apple, a comprehensive manual is included in the app which is effectively designed to get you up and running quickly.

03 Create your first presentation

Click the '+' icon at the bottom and then select New Presentation. You can choose from 12 themes, but for the purposes of this guide select the White one.

04 Build your first slide

On the first slide, double-tap the photo and tap the small icon that pops up. You can replace the photo with an image of your choice from the photo library.

05 Use your words

Double-tap the text and add your own words. When done, tap on the words and tap the 'i' icon. This will bring up a selection of styles and colours for the text.

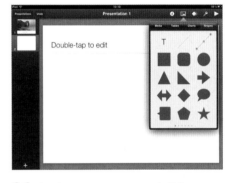

06 The important second slide

Tap the '+' icon on the bottom-left to create a second slide. Tap the picture icon at the top and then choose the 'Shapes' tab. Tap the 'T' to insert a new text box.

07 Add media

You will have noticed from the previous step that you are able to insert photographs, tables, charts and a variety of different shapes through the one command.

08 Time for tweaks

You can manipulate your media easily within Keynote. Tap a photograph and then hold two fingers on it – you can now spin it round to any angle you like.

09 Share your work

Once you have finished, you are able to share your work by tapping the left icon in the main document view. This will let you send it via email or to iWork.com.

App used:
AirPlay

Time needed:
10 minutes

Stream content with AirPlay

You can turn your iPad into your home media hub that all the family can share by streaming audio and video to other devices in your house. Here's how…

While it's great to be able to carry your favourite films, photos and music with you on your iPad, let's be honest: the joy is a personal one, as the iPad's speakers and screen are hardly built for sharing with a wider audience.

Or at least it would be without the iPad's killer feature: AirPlay. It allows you to stream your iPad's music, video and images wirelessly across a local network.

The only extra you need to use AirPlay is a compatible device to stream your iPad's content to. This could be an AppleTV, AirPlay-enabled stereo speakers – of which there are several on the market – or an AirPort Express wireless base station, which comes with a socket that enables it to connect to a home stereo system. A button tap is all it takes to free your audio and video and watch films on the big screen, or listen to your music collection on your best speakers. No wires required.

"A tap is all it takes to free your audio and video and watch films on a big screen"

AirPlay   Set up your AirPlay connection

01 Check wireless settings

AirPlay works over a local Wi-Fi network, so check that your iPad and the device you're streaming to are on the same network. You can set this up on the iPad by tapping Settings and choosing the Wi-Fi option. If your network is secured, you will need to enter its password.

02 Open the media

When your devices are properly connected, start playing the media on the iPad that you want to stream to another device. When you play a movie or a song on your iPad tap the AirPlay icon (a hollow rectangle with a solid triangle) that appears on the media controller.

AirPlay on the iPad in action

AirPlay is an impressive technology, but
it's pretty simple to use

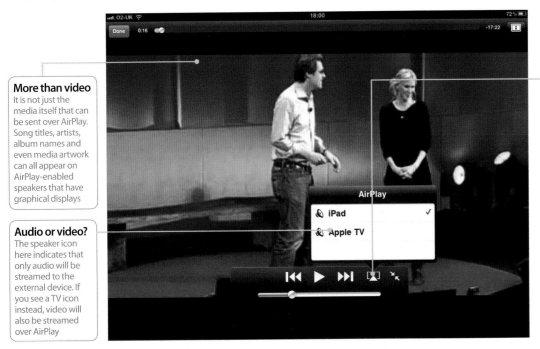

More than video
It is not just the
media itself that can
be sent over AirPlay.
Song titles, artists,
album names and
even media artwork
can all appear on
AirPlay-enabled
speakers that have
graphical displays

Audio or video?
The speaker icon
here indicates that
only audio will be
streamed to the
external device. If
you see a TV icon
instead, video will
also be streamed
over AirPlay

AirPlay's icon
The AirPlay icon itself is just a
simple box with an arrow. The
same icon appears on all iOS
devices, and in iTunes on the
Mac and PC too

AirPlay everywhere
AirPlay is a clever wireless
technology the usefulness of
which isn't restricted to the iPad.
In fact, any iOS device with iOS
4.2 or later installed on it can
use AirPlay – and so can the
iTunes application on Mac OSX.
AirPlay features are also present
in Apple's free Remote iPad and
iPhone app, which allows you to
control an iTunes library from an
iOS device. But not all video can
be streamed using AirPlay. At the
time of writing, video streaming
from the iPad is limited to media
that is streamed from Apple's
own apps – other apps can only
stream audio.

03 Choose your output

When you tap the AirPlay icon, a pop-up menu will appear, offering a choice
of AirPlay-enabled devices. The currently selected output displays a tick
next to it, and it should be your iPad. Tap the name of the device that you
would like to stream to.

04 Stream in action

Unfortunately, you are not able to watch the same video in two places at the
same time. Once you have selected another output device from the list, the
video or audio is sent there within just a couple of seconds. The iPad's screen
will then go blank!

The next step

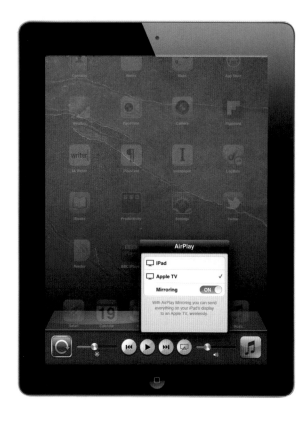

View iPad content on your Apple TV

If your iPad's screen isn't large enough, don't worry. With the help of Apple TV, you can use the big screen instead

 It's safe to say that video mirroring is one of the iPad 2's best kept secrets. It's so called because when activated, it mirrors the display of your iPad on a TV screen with the help of Apple TV.

That can have a number of obvious benefits. If you're tired of huddling around your iPad's screen when you share a video with your friends, you'll appreciate the ability to relax and view the video on a larger screen. Games take on a new dimension on the big screen, and some are even optimised for mirroring, showing the controls on your iPad, while the TV displays the action.

There are some limitations with video mirroring, though. For a start, mirroring isn't possible with the original iPad (you can't use it on iPod touches either, nor on iPhones before the iPhone 4S) and the iPad's aspect ratio doesn't match that of most TVs, so you'll probably see a black bar on either side of the screen. Some applications can display at full HD resolution, however.

The only other real drawback to video mirroring on your iPad is that it isn't always obvious how to turn it on. But that's something that's easy to address, and this tutorial's here to show you how to do it.

AirPlay Turn on video mirroring

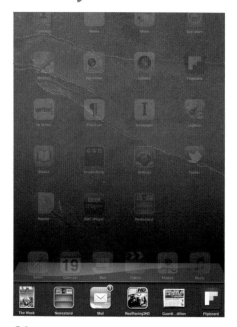

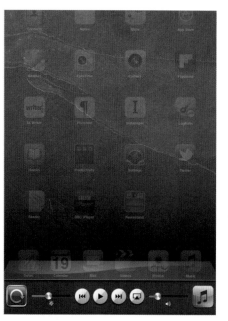

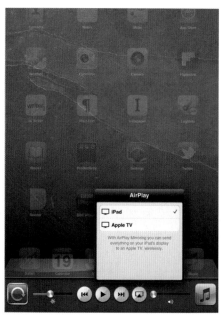

01 Set it up

The controls for video mirroring aren't found in the iPad's Settings. Instead, double-tap the Home button to bring up the iPad's multitasking bar, which shows your recently used apps.

02 Select your Apple TV

Swipe your finger to the right and you should see the AirPlay icon next to the iPod controls. Tap the icon and you should see any Apple TVs connected to your Wi-Fi network in the list.

03 Turn mirroring on

Tap 'Apple TV' in the list to select it and, underneath, slide the 'Mirroring' option to the 'On' position. In a second or two, the iPad's Home screen should be visible on your TV.

Setting up mirroring

Getting the best out of AirPlay

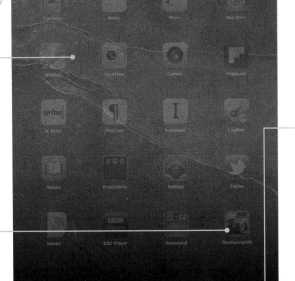

iPad rotation
The display on your TV screen mimics the rotation of your iPad, so you'll probably get better results by rotating your screen to landscape mode

Play your videos
To play an iPad video full-screen on your TV, tap the Videos app then tap the AirPlay icon

Newer iPads only
AirPlay only works on the second-generation Apple TV and on the latest iPads. Older devices just won't work

Using full screen
Some apps, such as Real Racing HD, will adjust their display to expand into full-screen on your TV

Mirroring with wires
Don't have an Apple TV or a wireless connection? Apple also sells an HDMI adapter cable that can link your iPad and TV directly through the latter's HDMI port. The results are as good as using AirPlay wirelessly, but of course, the cable will restrict your iPad's movements.

04 Run AirPlay
Now everything that appears on your iPad will also be displayed on the larger TV screen. As confirmation, the iPad's title bar turns blue and shows the Airplay icon.

05 Rotate the iPad
AirPlay will respect the aspect ratio of your iPad, so unless you're using a full-screen app, it won't fill the screen. But you can rotate the iPad and the rotation will change the display on the screen too.

06 Play streaming video
You can play streaming HTML video full screen by navigating to the video, then tapping the AirPlay icon that appears next to it. It will now expand to play on your TV screen.

App used:
AirPrint

 Time needed:
10 minutes

Print from your iPad with AirPrint

Yes, believe it or not, you can actually print from your iPad – but there are some tricks you should know first. Here are our secrets to iPad printing…

 When critics sought to find flaws in the iPad on its release last year, one weakness they focused on was its inability to print. At the time, for a permanent record of anything on your iPad's screen you had to email a copy to your Mac or PC and print it from there.

But the arrival of iOS 4.2 ended those complaints by bringing printing to the iPad's set of features. And in true Apple fashion it's a cinch to use – even if it does have limitations.

AirPrint works with most popular iPad applications, such as Pages, Safari and Photos. It works over a local Wi-Fi network, so in order to use it you need to be on the same network as the printer that you plan to use. The catch is that the iPad only prints to AirPrint-compatible printers, currently restricted to a limited range (a full list can be found at http://bit.ly/euwjbk). But the good news is that some third-party utilities enable you to print to any printer on your network.

> ## "AirPrint works with most popular iPad applications, such as Pages and Safari"

AirPrint How to print a webpage

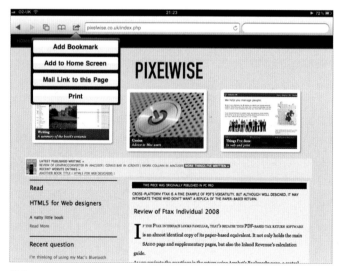

01 Choose the page to print

Many iPad apps now support printing, and most use the same technique. To print a page in Safari, for example, navigate to the page you want to print, click the arrow icon at the top of the screen, and select the Print option from the drop-down menu.

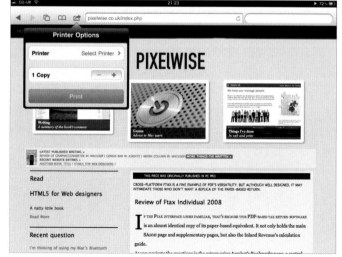

02 Choose the printer

Your iPad doesn't automatically know which printer you want to print to. The first time you print from an application, you will be prompted to select a printer. You will have to tap Select Printer to make your choice from the available printers.

Printing on the iPad

Most iPad apps follow the same approach when printing

Find the Print icon
In most apps that support printing, the printing option is found under the same 'arrow in box' icon

Options
Currently Apple restricts the type of printer you can print to, but here we're using the Printopia utility to print to a non-AirPrint-compatible Canon printer

Switching printers
The iPad remembers your chosen printer, but if you want to change the one you would like to use, tap the printer in the list and you will be taken to another drop-down menu showing all available options

Number of copies
Quickly choose the number of copies you would like to print by tapping the '+' or '-' buttons. Depending on the options that your printer supports, you may see additional choices here

Print to any printer
So what do you do if you don't have an AirPrint-ready printer? One way around this limitation is to use Printopia (**www.ecamm. com/mac/printopia**), a Mac utility that when installed lets your iPad print to any printer attached to your Mac, even it isn't AirPrint compatible. It also adds a 'virtual printer' that lets you send PDFs or JPEGs directly from your iPad straight to your Mac.

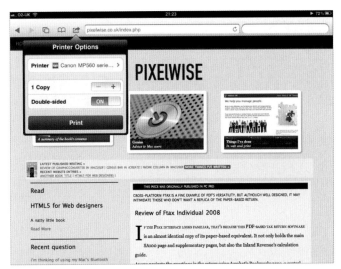

03 The printer list
As long as you're on the same Wi-Fi network as your printers, you should see every AirPrint-enabled device in this list. Choose the device that you would like to print the webpage to, so you can select any further printing options.

04 Choosing options
Depending on the printer you have selected, you may get other printing options. For example, if your printer supports double-sided printing, this may appear as an option. When you're happy with the options you have chosen, tap the 'Print' button and the page will be printed.

Tweet from your iPad

Follow the day-to-day activities of your favourite folk and share the latest news from your own life with this super social networking app

App used: Twitter

Time needed: 10 minutes

As you'll probably know by now, Twitter enables you to share short messages (no more than 144 characters in length) with the rest of the world – much like the status updates in Facebook. Even if you don't have a Twitter account it's impossible to avoid the influence of this social networking site. Politicians, banks and your favourite TV personality are more likely to have a Twitter account than not, so that they can update you on their latest activities.

The iPad Twitter app enables you to subscribe to – or follow – the Twitter broadcasts of particular people. You can also broadcast – or tweet – your own thoughts, and you may pick up some followers along the way who will hang off your every word.

To follow this tutorial you'll need to install the free Twitter app from the iTunes Store. Once you launch the app you can click Sign Up to create your own Twitter account, or Sign In if you've already got one. We'll then show you how to make your own tweets and find interesting people to follow.

> "Even if you don't have a Twitter account you can't avoid the influence of this site"

Twitter Start tweeting with this app

01 Set up a profile
To help future followers know who you are, click Profile, then Edit Profile. Click Profile Image to find a mug shot from your iPad's Photo Library – you'll need to use a small photo as Twitter doesn't like large files. Tap bio and write a brief description of yourself then click Save.

02 Make a tweet
To tweet, tap the icon at the screen's bottom left. Type into the New Tweet window. As you're limited to a message containing 144 characters, you'll see a countdown at the bottom left of the Tweet window. You can even attach a photo to the tweet. Click Send when you're ready.

Twitter in action

Get to know your way around the Twitter interface

Similar

This section provides an effective way of introducing you to new people to follow. If you're following a British comedian like Jimmy Carr, then you might enjoy keeping tabs on similar celebrities like Matt Lucas for example

Retweet

If you want to share someone's latest tweet with your own followers, click here and choose Retweet (or Quote Tweet) from the pop-up menu. This function enables particular news items or issues to get really amazing publicity

Timeline

When any of the people that you follow make a tweet, it will appear in this scrolling Timeline page. To find out more about a particular person simply click on their photo and their profile page will then appear just to the right of the Timeline

Make a tweet

Click here to open the New Tweet window. Tap out anything you want to share using the iPad's keyboard. Potential followers can find you if your tweet contains topics that they are searching for

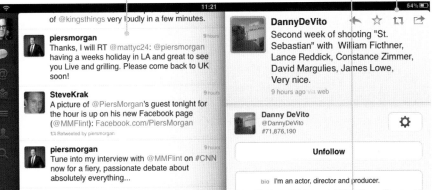

Twitter iOS 5 integration

When you update to iOS 5, Twitter will become integrated into a host of Apple apps to make it more convenient to tweet than ever before. You will still need to download and install the free Twitter app, but once done, go to Settings and then tap on the 'Twitter' section. From here you can allow apps such as Photos, Safari, YouTube, Camera and Maps to use your Twitter account. Once set-up, you will then be able to tweet quickly and easily from within those apps without even having to leave them.

03 Follow that star

To find folk to follow, click Search and type in a name. Each person's Twitter ID is prefaced with an @ symbol. If you want to follow the head writer of *Doctor Who*, for instance, then click on @steven_moffat to see their Twitter profile. Their bio should confirm that you've got the right person. Click Follow.

04 Explore

Once you've found people to follow click on the Timeline icon. The latest tweets from the people you follow will appear. Tap on a person's photo to see their profile. You can then click their Tweets icon to see all their recent tweets. Swipe the screen to move between various open profiles.

 App used:
Twitter

 Time needed:
5 minutes

How to make use of Twitter integration

With Twitter integrated into iOS 5, instantly share thoughts, feelings and links from your favourite apps

 There's little doubt that Twitter is a social phenomenon. This simple application allows you to share thoughts – or 'tweets' – with people around the world almost as soon as they enter your head, and likewise, see what's on the minds of people that you choose to follow.

The advent of smartphones has taken this concept to the next level by allowing you to tweet at any time, wherever you are in the world, making it easier than ever to speak your mind. Now, the tweeting process just got even easier with iOS 5.

Twitter is integrated seamlessly into Apple's new operating system; simply sign in, then begin tweeting directly from your favourite apps. You no longer need to open a specific Twitter app, find a photo to upload or copy links from your web browser; simply do it directly from within the app. It's so easy that your Twitter activity will increase dramatically once you get to grips with it. In this tutorial, we guide you through setting up Twitter integration, and how to tweet from your favourite apps.

"Share your thoughts with the world and see what's on your friends' minds"

Twitter Tweet from within your favourite apps

01 Go to Settings

Choose Settings, then tap on the Twitter option in the left-hand column. If you don't already have Twitter installed, tap Install.

02 Log in

Enter your details – including your username and password – adjust the 'Find Me by Email' and Tweet Location options, and tap Done.

03 Tweet in Safari

Open Safari. To tweet about a page, tap the Add Bookmark option, and choose Tweet. A link to the page will be added to your tweet.

Integrating Twitter

Tweet easily from other apps

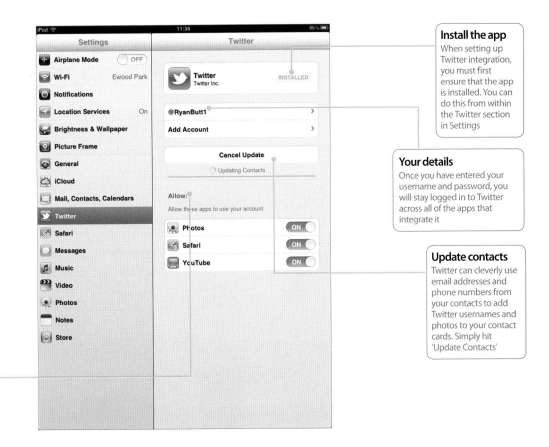

Install the app
When setting up Twitter integration, you must first ensure that the app is installed. You can do this from within the Twitter section in Settings

Your details
Once you have entered your username and password, you will stay logged in to Twitter across all of the apps that integrate it

Update contacts
Twitter can cleverly use email addresses and phone numbers from your contacts to add Twitter usernames and photos to your contact cards. Simply hit 'Update Contacts'

Camera comments
If your iPhone 4 or iPad 2 device has iOS 5 installed, then you can also tweet from within the Camera app, allowing you to upload, comment and caption your pictures almost as soon as they are captured. Keeping others informed of your actions has never been so easy.

Grant permissions
In order to allow Twitter to become integrated with other apps, you must grant permission for particular apps to use your Twitter account

04 Tweet in Photos
When viewing an image, tap the share icon, and select Tweet. Any pictures you tweet about will be added as a link to your message.

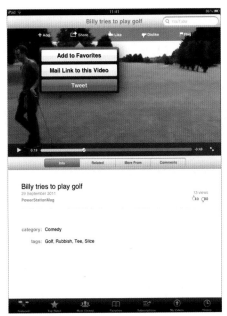

05 Tweet in YouTube
Share videos in YouTube by tapping the Share button at the top of the viewing window, then Tweet. A link will be added to your message.

06 Tweet in Maps
Tweet your current location or places of interest by tapping on your current location, then the 'i' icon. Choose Share Location, then Tweet.

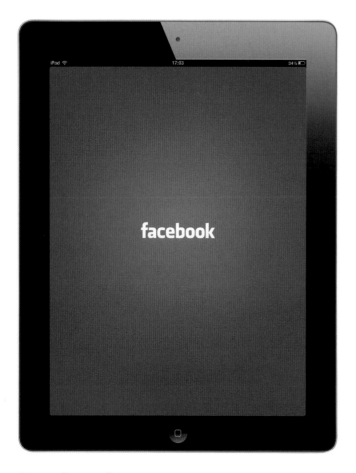

 App used:
Facebook

 Time needed:
5 minutes

Find your way around the Facebook app

If you have a Facebook account and don't want to bother using Safari to access it, there's an app that makes it much more compact. Here's how to use it

It may have taken a while but finally Facebook has come to the iPad. No longer will you need to use the iPhone app and zoom in, or log-in through Safari, everything is now neatly organised and on-hand. The main advantage of the app is that it is very well organised and easier to use than the actual website, and on top of that, the app uses notifications to let you know immediately about responses to your actions, posts on your wall or requests from friends.

Once the Facebook app is downloaded and installed on your iPad, you simply need to enter your email address and Facebook password to get going. So now let's go see some of the functions that make accessing your account on the move as much fun as the main site.

"The app is very well organised and easier to use than the website"

Facebook Get friendly with this iPad app

01 Get started

The first step will be to download the app from the App Store. Upon opening the app for the first time, you will need to enter your email address and password to access your existing account, or if you don't have one you can create a new account.

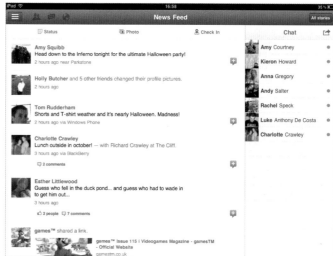

02 Live news feeds

You will now be taken straight to the Live News feed page. This will show you all the updates from your friends, and from here you can also see who is online to chat. You can gain access to all the other areas of the app from the top bar too.

Staying up to date on Facebook

Here's all the features that revolve around your personal profile

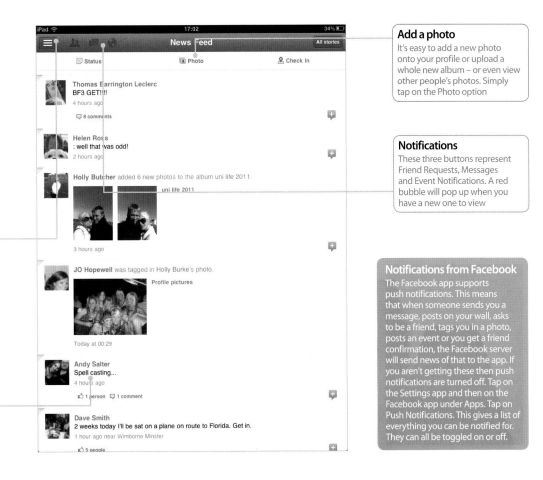

Add a photo
It's easy to add a new photo onto your profile or upload a whole new album – or even view other people's photos. Simply tap on the Photo option

Notifications
These three buttons represent Friend Requests, Messages and Event Notifications. A red bubble will pop up when you have a new one to view

Info pane
Tap on this button to bring up the pane that will allow you to access your personal page, or view events, friends, messages and much more

News Feed
This page is the main news feed and will keep you up to date with everything going on. From here you can Like or Dislike stories, or add your own comments with ease

Notifications from Facebook
The Facebook app supports push notifications. This means that when someone sends you a message, posts on your wall, asks to be a friend, tags you in a photo, posts an event or you get a friend confirmation, the Facebook server will send news of that to the app. If you aren't getting these then push notifications are turned off. Tap on the Settings app and then on the Facebook app under Apps. Tap on Push Notifications. This gives a list of everything you can be notified for. They can all be toggled on or off.

03 Post your status
The very first option along the top bar allows you to post your status. Simply tap on the 'Status' link and a new box will open. You can then type away, add an image and also tag the location you are currently in. Once your status is complete, simply tap 'Post'.

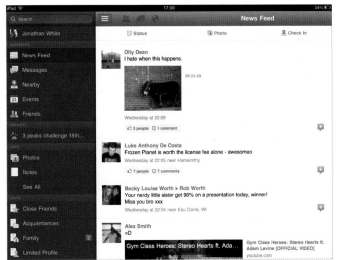

04 The main hub
The box at the top-left with the three lines brings up a pane of options. From here you can access your personal home page, view events, messages, friends and much more. When you're done, simply swipe the pane back to hide it.

100 Essential Apps

Sort the wheat from the chaff with this comprehensive guide to the must-own apps for your iPad

The writer Theodore Sturgeon coined the adage '90 per cent of everything is crud'. As the Apple App Store has thousands of apps to choose from, it can be a daunting task to decide which ones to download, especially if you have to fork out your hard-earned cash.

This feature should help you fill your iPad with apps that are useful, informative and perhaps even life-saving! To help you find 'keepers' for your iPad, we'll give you an overview of the App Store's 20 categories and highlight five 'must-have apps' from each one.

We'll unveil apps to keep you occupied and entertained, apps that turn reluctant cooks into credible chefs, apps that let non-musicians make sweet sounds, and apps to give you local knowledge even if you're in a strange neighbourhood. Having the right apps on your iPad can transform your life in many ways, so read on to discover which ones we recommend and why.

5 essential apps

01 iBooks

Price: Free **Developer:** Apple

iBooks is the closest thing you'll need to reading a 'real' book without feeling guilty about killing a tree. The pages curl as you drag to turn them over and your collection of books is displayed on a bookshelf. You can download sample chapters of most books to try before you buy, change the font size and find words or phrases with a quick search, which is faster than looking through a hard copy's index.

02 Kindle

Price: Free **Developer:** AMZN Mobile LLC

Kindle was initially a handheld digital book-reading tablet invented by Amazon. By downloading the free Kindle app you can turn your gadget into a Kindle reader with ease (which saves you the expense of buying the dedicated digital book reader). You can use Kindle to shop for books at the Amazon store and download books on the spot. This saves you the hassle of waiting for the postman to deliver books in time for your holiday's departure date!

03 Ladybird Classic Me Books

Price: £0.69/$0.99 **Developer:** Penguin Books

This is an enthralling app for kids and a must-have nostalgic trip back in time for adults. Through this reading portal app you can purchase and download a wide range of classic Ladybird books, with their original covers and illustrations and then read through them with memory-induced tears in your eyes. It's not all old-school though because you can record audio segments for your kids to tap on and even get the whole story narrated by a famous voice. Classic.

04 Alice for the iPad **Price:** £5.99/$8.99

Developer: Atomic Antelope

This is Lewis Carroll's classic tale touched by technology for a fantastic and memorable interactive reading experience. Revisit the story, iPad style, with fully-animated scenes that embrace the device's tilt technology to stunning effect. The are 52 lush pages to explore and plenty to delight children.

05 Comics

Price: Free **Developer:** comiXology

The iPad is perfect for reading comics and this app's Guided View technology helps you pan and zoom from panel to panel in a tap. This is quicker than having to swipe or pinch. There are many free comics to download (and you can preview a few pages of the paid editions). Essential for comic fans of all ages.

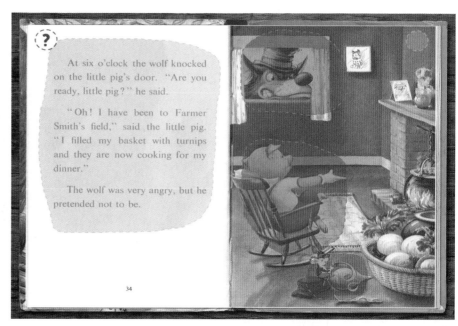

■ In Ladybird Classic Me Books you can tap on words and pictures to record your own audio segments

■ You can purchase a selection of classic books from within the app…

Books

Before we owned an iPad, planning our holiday reading could be a bit of a dilemma. We'd need enough books to keep us occupied while lounging on a sunbed for a week or two, but were limited by what we could cram into our suitcase. This reduced our reading list to a few paperbacks. Thanks to today's electronic book apps we can download hundreds of books onto our iPad without eating into our luggage's weight or space allowance! This gives us more than enough material to read on the plane, before bed and on the beach. Indeed the holiday will be over before we can finish our downloaded novels.

When it comes to books there's an app for everyone. You can download your favourite author's

"When it comes to books there's an app for everyone"

latest epic, catch up on the classics for free and keep the tiny tots entertained with illustrated storybooks. There are even comic book apps to keep superhero fans happy!

■ Alice for iPad contains lots scenes to interact with…

■ It is easy to find gripping reads in the Comics app…

■ Build up your own space-saving digital collection!

Business

Your iPad isn't just for playing games or reading books – it means Business too! There's a whole category on the App Store dedicated to turning your iPad into a valuable business tool. Time is money, so we've highlighted five essential apps that will speed up typical work chores like quickly recording all of your spontaneous thoughts and ideas and transcribing them into text, creating, editing and sharing Microsoft Word, Excel and PowerPoint files, accessing your office computer desktop from anywhere in the world, viewing and editing PDF files on the move and, thanks to the two-way cameras on the iPad 2, attend important meetings without leaving your home. Our essential apps will enable you to spend less time in the office and more time at play.

"Spend less time in the office and more time at play"

■ Dragon Dictation is a great app for capturing thoughts…

■ WebEx has an introductory video to guide you through the app

■ Dragon Dictation is easy to use – just tap to record

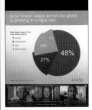

■ With WebEx you can attend virtual board meetings

■ Documents To Go lets you create and edit all Microsoft Office documents on your iPad…

5 essential apps

01 Dragon Dictation
Price: Free
Developer: Nuance Communications

You may never have had a personal secretary to type up your words of wisdom, but thanks to this app you can enjoy watching your speech turn to text. Simply tap the record button and chat into your gadget's microphone. If it makes mistakes, then you can summon the keyboard and fine-tune. Once you've created some text then it's a doddle to send it to Facebook or Twitter with a tap. With practise this app could be a genuine time-saver.

02 Documents To Go
Price: £6.99/$9.99 **Developer:** DataViz, Inc

Anyone who has reservations about trading their laptop in for an iPad should dispel such concerns now because this versatile app allows you to access your Microsoft Office files at any time and view, edit and create new documents on the move. These files can then be transferred wirelessly between your office computer and your device for ease of access and piece of mind while working remotely. Sturdy, reliable and easy to use, this is a sound investment.

03 Wyse PocketCloud Pro
Price: £10.49/$14.99 **Developer:** Wyse Tech

This app is a secure and fast way to remotely connect to your Mac or Windows desktop with your iPad, no matter where you are. Access your files and applications, like Outlook Express, Word, Photoshop, and build your own personal cloud to store all of your important files. It's simple to use and with powerful features, enterprise security and RDP/VNC compatibility, is a great device for helping you work remotely with ease.

04 WebEx for iPad
Price: Free **Developer:** Cisco

Steer clear of those stuffy boardrooms but never miss a meeting with this great app. With an iPad 2 you get two-way video on your device to ensure that you can engage and interact with your colleagues, even if you aren't there in a physical sense.

05 PDF Reader Pro
Price: £3.99/$5.99
Developer: Po-chou Su

This feature-rich app lets you render and view PDFs quickly as well as annotate them, apply sticky notes and highlight specific areas. The latest update also allows you to convert files to PDFs from within the app. A great app for all of your viewing and editing needs.

Essential apps

■ Bloomberg keeps you informed and up to date

Finance

In these tight times it pays to watch your pennies – and you can do that with help from these essential apps from the iTunes Finance category. They will help you avoid being ripped off when converting your currency for a trip abroad or enable you to work out how expensive a road trip will be when filling up your car with petrol. We'll also feature apps designed to help you keep track of your daily expenses, so that you can enjoy spending money while keeping your account safely in the black. There are also apps that allow you to keep up to date with all the latest share prices and read up on all the latest financial news. There is definitely something to suit everyone in the Finance category of the App Store and, by way of a bonus, many of the apps are totally free, which is always helpful.

2011-12-19 15:59:38:Expedition 30 Soyuz Rolls to the Pad. SOURCE:NASA Baikonur Cosmodrome, Kazakhstan, Monday, Dec. 19, 2011. The launch of Engineer Don Pettit and European Space Agency astronaut and Flight Engin NASA/Carla Cioffi Mission: International space station For credit and copyr

Browse All Mode
2011-12-19 : 12 of 1833

■ Learn all about what NASA does with this free app…

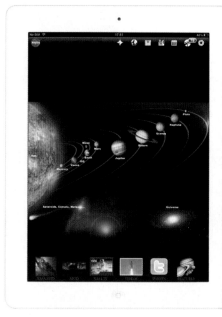

■ Learn more about the universe with NASA app HD

■ Track your finances easily with Pocket Money

■ The iCurrency app is great for staying within budget

Education

The iPad is the perfect platform to help you develop your knowledge of a wide range of subjects. Regardless of your age, there's an app to suit everyone. Babies can be stimulated by simple cause and effect when they tap the screen to trigger pictures and relevant sound effects and toddlers can be entertained and educated by story-telling apps that they can interact with by triggering animations with a tap or swipe. Seasoned stargazers can use apps to identify stars and constellations in the night sky or explore the wonders of the universe via images of space captured by the orbiting Hubble telescope. In this section we also recommend good apps to use in the classroom when teaching and apps to enthuse, engage and entertain you when you need a little extra inspiration.

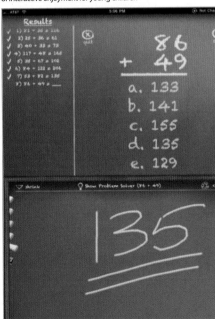
■ The Wheels on the Bus HD app provides plenty of interactive enjoyment for young children

■ Attend engaging and insightful seminars conducted by a wide range of inspiring people with the TED app

■ Learn all about sums quickly with MathBoard

■ TED holds a plethora of useful talks for you to be informed by

5 essential apps

01 Star Walk for iPad

Price: £2.99/$4.99 **Developer:** Vito Technology
This interstellar app places a Planetarium in your hands. By holding your iPad 2 up against the sky you'll see a computer generated map of the heavens (day or night!). As you scan the heavens, Star Walk overlays graphics that give you extra information. Lines join stars together to indicate constellations, and symbols overlay the relevant stars. The search function pinpoints objects with ease, whether they are distant planets or orbiting satellites.

02 Wheels on the Bus HD

Price: £1.49/$2.99 **Developer:** Duck Duck Moose
This interactive songbook features characters and objects that react to a toddler's tap. As the title song is sung, kids can push the school bus along the screen with their fingers, swipe to open the doors or poke various characters to make them jump! This app will keep your little ones entertained.

03 NASA App HD

Price: Free **Developer:** NASA Ames Research
This free app is an insightful gaze to the stars alongside the NASA space program and includes live streaming of NASA TV, mission information, satellite tracking, Twitter feeds, maps and links to all of the NASA centers and much more. Anyone with even the slightest interest in our solar system would be well advised to check this out as it is well produced with a slick and stylish interface and overflowing with content.

04 TED

Price: Free **Developer:** TED Conferences
This app is a database of insightful, informative talks by some of the world's most influential people across a wide range of fields, the aim being to be enthralled and inspired by experts in the field of economics, technology, agriculture, business and more. Movies can be viewed on iPad or on your TV via AirPlay.

05 MathBoard

Price: £2.99/$4.99 **Developer:** Paul Schmitt
Anyone struggling with sums would be well-advised to download this brainbox of an app. This is essentially an effective learning tool for learning all aspects of maths packed into an engaging and intuitive interface. It also comes packed with quizzes to ensure all learnt info stays learnt.

Essential apps

■ The BBC iPlayer app is great for catching up on missed TV

Entertainment

Thanks to your ever-present iPad there's no danger that you'll get bored on long journeys (or when sitting on the loo!), especially if you pack it with essential apps from the Entertainment category of the App Store. You can use apps to help you keep tabs on what's on the telly so that you don't miss a thing, or enjoy interactive TV spin-off apps featuring your favourite characters. You can entertain family and friends with a variety of funny or even scary apps. In the following section we'll show you apps that help you record your favourite TV programmes on the move, have fun playing with your photo collection, create professional-looking works of art and see what's on at the cinemas local to where you are (and read up on what's hot and what's pants in the world of cinema). Whatever your entertainment tastes there should be something here to keep you occupied for hours on end.

■ Unleash your inner creativity with Sketchbook Pro

■ Have fun morphing pictures with FaceGoo HD…

■ The Sky+ app allows you to record TV on the move

5 essential apps

01 BBC iPlayer
Price: Free
Developer: Media App

 This was the original TV catch up viewing portal app released on the iPad and it is still the best. This could be largely thanks to the diverse selection of programmes on offer, which range from insightful documentaries to great comedy and sport, but the interface is so easy to use and well produced that finding things to watch is a quick and easy process.

02 Sketchbook Pro for iPad
Price: £2.99/$4.99
Developer: Autodesk

 This app delivers a complete set of sketching and painting tools through a streamlined and intuitive user interface that is based on the professional-grade desktop app, but designed exclusively for the iPad experience. Whether you're a professional illustrator or occasional doodler, this is the perfect app for getting creative.

03 Sky+
Price: Free
Developer: BSkyB

 This is an essential app for all Sky+ users as it not only provides full listings for all Sky channels, it also allows you to remotely hit 'record' on your Sky+ box and save what you want, even if you're on the other side of the world. You can also group channel favourites together to create your very own personal TV guide. A great innovative app for Sky users on the go.

04 Flixter
Price: Free
Developer: Flixster

 Wherever you are in the country, this app will use your iPad's GPS feature to find the current films showing at your nearest cinemas (which you can locate using Maps). If you're stuck for inspiration about what to see, view trailers and read reviews of a particular film so you can avoid wasting money (or wait for the DVD release). A must-have app for film fans!

05 FaceGoo HD
Price: £1.99/$2.99
Developer: Robot Wheelie

 This fun, distracting app lets you manipulate and morph pictures in to grotesque parodies. You can use the preloaded portraits or import your own images and the effects that you can apply with your fingers are incredible – simply swipe your finger to start distorting and apply all manner of scars and boils.

5 essential apps

01 Infinity Blade
Price: £3.99/$5.99
Developer: Chair Ent

 Simple in concept – you traverse the same dungeons over and over again gaining enough XP and dough to buy the better weapons needed to defeat the hulking knights you face. Great controls, amazing graphics and endless replay value, this game is an iPad benchmark – and the good news it has recently spawned a sequel that allows you to explore dark new realms and face even harder enemies.

02 World Of Goo HD
Price: £2.99/$4.99
Developer: 2D BOY

 This quirky puzzle game has you pulling and plying balls of goo to shape structures and defences to conquer the many levels. This cute, curious game is brimming with personality and features some stunning visual effects. The game also features a massive online competition where goo-getters battle on a live leaderboard to build the tallest tower of goo. Fun for all the family.

03 Angry Birds HD
Price: £2.99/$4.99
Developer: Chillingo Ltd

 This entertaining platform and puzzle game deserves a place on every iPad. Use a catapult to fire a variety of birds through the air to topple objects and kill enemies hiding behind them. Different birds have different abilities – tap on a bird to make it speed up or even explode. Be warned – its combination of addictive play and high production values can eat your spare time up.

04 Plants Vs Zombies HD
Price: £4.99/$6.99
Developer: PopCap Games

 This tower defense game has you protecting your home against multiple waves of shambling zombies. You'll have to act fast and plan ahead to keep them from your door while using sunlight to fuel your fauna army. As you progress you'll unlock new wacky plants to line-up and delay or disintegrate the decaying hordes. Just brilliant.

05 Order & Chaos Online
Price: £4.99/$6.99
Developer: Gameloft

 This is the iPad's premier real-time full 3D MMORPG that places players into a graphically-rich and diverse fantasy world to play alongside thousands of other adventurers. You can lose yourself in this for weeks on end. You are provided with a three-month subscription upon download but after that you pay to play.

Games

The iPad is a gamer's dream come true. Its high-quality screen displays pixels perfectly so you can enjoy a game's colours and graphics to the full. It's more than capable of pushing pixels around at a decent frame rate so the action never falters. Unlike traditional handheld consoles, iPad games are relatively cheap (or even free for lite 'try before you buy' versions), so you'll never be short of games to enjoy. Gameplay varies dramatically, from first-person shooters to exhilarating sports platform games. The iPad's touch screen makes it possible to play games without a joypad – and many apps make good use of this feature. Some games also put the iPad's accelerometer to good use so that you can steer characters by simply tilting the device. Whatever style of game you favour there's sure to be something to take your fancy in our essential roundup, right here.

■ Even life in the distant reaches of the galaxy have played Angry Birds…

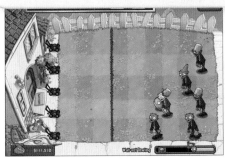

■ Plants Vs Zombies is insanely addictive…

■ Take your fight online with Order & Chaos

■ Infinity Blade – has to be seen to be believed

Health & Fitness

We all make plans to stay fitter and thinner at various times (especially in the new year with resolutions to be made), though our motivation often runs out of steam. However, with the right apps on your iPad you should be able to see a real change in your fitness level each day. For starters there are apps designed to help you to record and reduce your calorie intake, enabling you to lose weight at a pace that suits you, as well as highlighting flaws in your current diet. We'll even show you how to turn your iPad into high-tech barcode scanner that reads the amount of calories in the food you intend to buy and tells you if it's healthy or not. In case of accidents you can turn to apps for advice, and perform life-saving first aid if necessary. Need a symptom diagnosed? There is an app for that too. Needless to say our essential apps will provide you with guidance and advice, but they're no substitute for seeking a professional in a medical emergency. Here we recommend a great selection of apps for staying in shape and learning more about your body.

■ The Weight Watchers app is great for connecting you with other members and finding a meeting nearby

■ iFitness lets you track your food intake

■ Get fit with the iFitness app's help

5 essential apps

01 Fitness for iPad
Price: £0.69/$0.99
Developer: Arawella Corp

This feature-heavy app provides you with hundreds of fitness exercises and yoga poses, 40 complete workouts, a calorie counter, body tracker and plenty of extra tools for helping you get into shape and monitor your fitness. It is a friendly, informative app that is easy to follow and packed with information to help you keep in shape. The price is very enticing too.

02 Army Survival for iPad/iPhone
Price: £1.49/$2.99
Developer: Double Dog

This digital field manual is the most authoritative survival guide available on iPad and comes packed with over 1,400 pages rammed with tricks of the trade for staying alive while out in the wild. This is a fascinating and insightful read that is well-presented and easy-to-follow thanks to neat diagrams and plenty of information across a wide range of topics.

03 Food Scanner: Good Food or Bad Food?
Price: £1.99/$2.99
Developer: Arawella Corp

If you're into healthy eating and treat your body like a temple, this app is designed to help you make informed choices on what you eat. Simply use the cameras on your iPad 2 scan the barcodes on food and the app determines if it's good or bad for you. Okay so it's a big part gimmick, but it's still a useful app that is great for showing off your device while helping up stay in shape.

04 iMuscle – (NOVA Series) – iPad Edition
Price: £2.99/$4.99
Developer: 3D4Medical.com

Through this app you can identify a body part or individual muscle by zooming in on a 3D diagram of the human body and then access a host of exercises associated with the development or rehabilitation of that particular muscle. It's a great tool as a teaching aid for fitness instructors and is an impressively detailed app.

05 Weight Watchers Mobile UK
Price: Free
Developer: Weight Watchers

If you're a member of the Weight Watchers program or simply fancy staying in shape then this app is just the dish. It features daily recipes, allows you to create shopping lists based on the recipes provided, find a meeting time and location near to where you are and connect with the community. It's a great little app that could really help you on your weight loss journey.

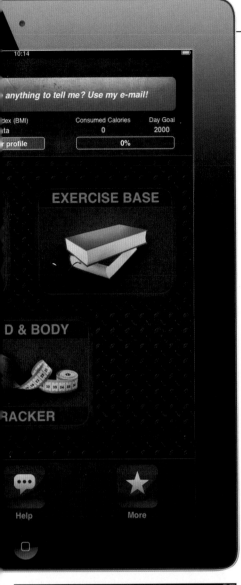

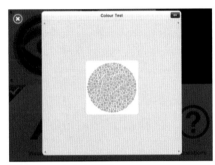

■ The Grays Anatomy app is packed with medical insight and is a great learning aid for students

■ Test your eyes for free with the Vision Test app

Medical

The Medical category of the App Store contains apps that complement the ones in the Health & Fitness section, so you're spoiled for choice when it comes to finding apps to help you stay fit and well. Some of the best apps in this category are detailed and insightful reference guides that will prove invaluable for medical students and anyone working in the field of medicine, but there is also a very wide selection of self-help aids to monitor blood pressure, units of alcohol, sugar levels and so on – so if you suffer from a particular affliction, then you're sure to find an app that will help you monitor and cope with your condition. There are also some very good eye-testing apps available that let you assess your peepers in the comfort of your own home to determine if you should get yourself down to the opticians for a proper test.

■ The Medical Oxford Dictionary app is expensive, but worth it

5 essential apps

01 Vision Test

Price: Free **Developer:** 3 Sided Cube Design

If you have a somewhat casual approach to getting your eyes tested regularly then Vision Test is a decent gauge for testing if your peepers are in need of a professional examination. It includes a Visual Acuity Test, Astigmatism Test, Duochrome Test, Colour Test and Far Field Vision Test, as well as an optician finder, advice and facts and a quiz to test your knowledge. It's totally free too!

02 Grays Anatomy Premium

Price: £2.99/$4.99 **Developer:** Luke Allen

First published in 1858 and considered by many to the one of the most iconic and significant medical books of all time, Grays Anatomy is now available on the iPad and grabs the technology with both hands to present its information in engaging new ways, accompanied by high-resolution images. It's a great, insightful source of information that will be invaluable to trainee doctors and nurses.

03 Medical Oxford Dictionary

Price: £10.49/$15.99
Developer: Handmark, Inc

This illustrated dictionary contains 12,500 authoritative entries on all aspects of medical science and is complimented by over 140 illustrations. Written and updated regularly by a dedicated team of medical experts, this is a great reference app for all things medical related that will prove invaluable to medical students and anyone working in medicine.

04 The Human Body

Price: £2.99/$4.99 **Developer:** Amber Books

A very cool app that describes 300 parts of the human anatomy through detailed illustrations and annotations. Each entry can be zoomed in on for extra scrutiny and the expert writers keep the info concise and accessible. A worthwhile and cheaper alternative to the wealth of in-depth references guides available.

05 Anatomy 3D: Organs

Price: £4.99/$6.99 **Developer:** Real Bodywork

Expand your knowledge of the human organs with this robust app that combines 3D models, video, audio lectures, quizzes and detail and descriptive text to create a rich learning experience. Well produced and thoroughly insightful, this app is great value for money and thoroughly absorbing.

■ Discover healthy recipes with the Weight Watchers app

5 essential apps

01 The Photo Cookbook

Price: £2.99/$4.99 **Developer:** ditter. projektagentur Gmb

 The Photo Cook Book – Quick and Easy does what it says on the tin! If you want to develop some culinary skills, then the lavishly illustrated Photo Cookbook is a must have. This educational app is packed full of recipes that guide you step-by-step. There's a wide range of dishes and desserts to create. You can also refer to a photo of a meal's raw ingredients when you're out shopping, so that you don't miss a thing!

02 Tesco Recipes

Price: Free **Developer:** Tesco PLC

 This fine free app provides plenty of culinary inspiration and allows you to purchased and get delivered all the ingredients you need to make your feast of fancy. The app is quick and easy to use and you can store all of the recipes that you like as favourites to access later and the app will sync to your computer, so you can start shopping for ingredients on one device and then continue on another.

03 eBay for iPad

Price: Free **Developer:** eBay Inc

 If you're a keen eBay user then this app is all you need to keep track of your online auctions. It's formatted for your iPad screen, so whether you're buying or selling you can find the information you need with ease. It can be a chore to leave feedback on multiple auctions or mark items as having been dispatched. Thanks to this fab app you can perform these tedious tasks on the move and stay on top of your eBay admin.

04 AroundMe

Price: Free **Developer:** Tweakersoft

 Every iPad needs an app that displays local amenities, and this one does the job effectively. Scroll through a list of categories (like Parking) and see a list of all the options (with the closest listed first). A quick tap will show the location on a map in relation to your own position.

05 Amazon Windowshop

Price: Free **Developer:** Amazon Eurasia

 As good as the Amazon website, but this app has been built around the iPad technology to provide a quick and easy shopping service. Searching for items and making quick purchases has never been so satisfying and everything is well laid out, easy to find and there is plenty of info provided on each and every item.

Lifestyle

The Lifestyle category of the App Store contains apps covering a diverse range of subjects. If you're keen on getting out and about (whether that's through walking or cycling), then you can use apps to map your favourite routes and discover how long a particular journey is in miles. While on a stroll you can fire up apps to help you discover local amenities (like pubs or restaurants), or check out the status of your eBay auctions when you're on the move. If you want to conquer your lack of cooking skills then we have a must-have app that will enable you to impress family and friends with newfound cooking skills and shop for essential ingredients (or pretty much anything else, for that matter). Whatever your lifestyle, you are sure to find apps that will make a difference to how you live your life.

"Whatever lifestyle, these apps should make a difference"

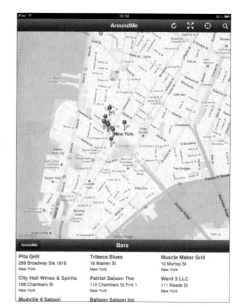

■ Discover the world around you with AroundMe

■ The eBay app is great for shopping and completing fiddly admin on the move…

 ■ Amazon Windowshop lets you find the product you want in a flash

 ■ Rustle up something special for dinner with the Tesco Recipes app

5 essential apps

01 Bloom HD
Price: £2.49/$3.99
Developer: Opal Limited

 A hypnotic, ambient app in which you create sound patterns by tapping different parts of the screen. It works brilliantly and you can create some great-sounding multi-layered pieces of music within minutes thanks to the simple interface. Developed by ambient pioneer Brian Eno and musician Peter Chivers, the quality shines through.

02 djay
Price: £6.99/$10.99
Developer: algoriddim

 This app is amazing – it looks lovely and functions fabulously. It places two vinyl turntables on your iPad's screen. You can place tracks from your iTunes library onto each turntable and play the tracks as if they were vinyl. A fader enables you to mix the two records together to create something new. You can mix live, or record and share your mix with mates.

03 TuneIn Radio Pro
Price: £0.69/$0.99
Developer: Synsion Radio Technologies

 Most radio stations these days also broadcast via the web, which is why TuneIn Radio Pro can find any radio station. You can set up a list of favourite stations and if something takes your fancy you can record. It'll even use your location to present you with a list of local stations. You'll never be short of something to listen to again with this great app!

04 Shazam for iPad
Price: Free
Developer: Shazam Entertainment Ltd.

 Hear a song you like but have no idea which band performs it? With Shazam you can whip out your iPad, let it listen to the music and identify the track in moments. You can discover song lyrics, see album covers and download the track via iTunes. This is definitely a musical must have for every iPad user with an interest in the latest tunes.

05 Amplitube for iPad
Price: £13.99/$16.99
Developer: IK Multimedia US, LLC

Used in conjunction with the iRig interface adaptor, AmpliTube allows you to transform your iPad into a feature-heavy electric guitar amp by plugging in your guitar and utilising a host of pedal effects. Brilliant if you can't afford a Marshall, this is one way to keep the neighbours happy.

Music

If you love listening to music, or even want to make it, then the following essential apps deserve a place on your iPad. We'll feature an amazing app that enables you to mix the Music library's tracks together like an old-school DJ (complete with scratchy back spins that you can produce by swiping the iPad's screen!). Alternatively you may want to simply stroke the screen to generate synthesized sounds and create a relaxing ambient soundscape – there's an app for that too! If you'd rather consume music than create it, then there's an app that will tell you the track and artist that you're listening to by sampling it through your iPad's mic, so you won't miss out on discovering new bands. You can rediscover old music too by listening to music-streaming apps, and turn your iPad into a radio that will pick up (and even record) stations from anywhere in the world.

■ Make some noise with the roadie-friendly Amplitube app

■ Shazam will have no trouble identifying songs for you to buy

■ Become a virtual DJ in the clever djay app

■ Make sweet sounds with the easy-to-use Bloom HD app...

Essential apps

5 essential apps

01 CoPilot Live HD

Price: £26.99/$39.99 **Developer:** ALK
Technologies, LTD.

This is the most expensive app in our
feature, but it's much cheaper than
buying a dedicated satnav. It uses your
iPad's GPS function to help you navigate road
trips. Like other satnav displays, you can see your
vehicle's position on a 3D map and follow arrows
that guide you. When you get to complex junctions
a lane indicator keeps you on track. It's worth
buying a hands-free mount holder so you don't get
distracted holding your gadget.

02 Layar Reality Browser

Price: Free **Developer:** Layar B.V.

Instead of using a 2D map to find local
points of interest, try a bit of augmented
reality! Layar works by allowing you to
search for a particular amenity (like a coffee shop).
Instead of displaying the search results as icons
on a 2D map it overlays them on your iPad 2's live
camera image. As you pan the device to view a
location you'll see floating icons or images that
represent the locations of your search results.

03 Trails – GPS tracker

Price: £2.49/$3.99 **Developer:** Felix Lamouroux

If you're a big fan of hiking then this
app will let you record your adventures
using the iPad's GPS facility. You can snap
photos of interesting sights along the way and
create waypoints to mark points of interest. Cyclists
should find this app useful to as it can display the
topography of the terrain. You can also download
maps before you set out in case the iPad can't get a
signal on your journey.

04 ForeverMap

Price: £1.49/$2.99 **Developer:** skobbler GmbH

If you're travelling abroad it can cost a
fortune to download map details using
the standard Maps app. ForeverMap lets
you download a country or city's map before you
travel so you can avoid excessive data roaming
charges. You can then use the downloaded map to
plan routes and discover points of interest.

05 Plane Finder HD

Price: £4.99/$6.99 **Developer:** pinkfroot limited

This fascinating real-time plane-tracking
app is a real eye-opener, as you can see
just how full our skies are with aircraft. If
your friends or family are travelling by air you can
follow their progress by searching for their flight
number. An essential app for any flight enthusiast.
There's a cut-down free version available too.

Navigation

We tend to carry our iPad around with us at all
times, so it's the perfect device to help us get where
we want to go, or find local amenities like pubs
or hotels. Your iPad already comes with a decent
built-in Maps app that does a great job of showing
you how to get from A to B – but there are other
apps that can extend and expand your gadget's
navigational abilities in exciting ways. In this
section we'll introduce you to five essential
navigation apps that perform a variety of different
functions. One of them even transforms your iPad
into a turn-by-turn navigator at the fraction of the
price of a dedicated gadget like a TomTom satnav
– just make sure you use it safely in the car. You can
also keep tabs on the flight paths of specific planes,
or discover the location of local points of interest by
panning the iPad 2's camera around the area you
are in.

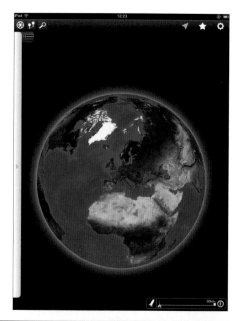

■ ForeverMap could save you a lot of
money while you're travelling

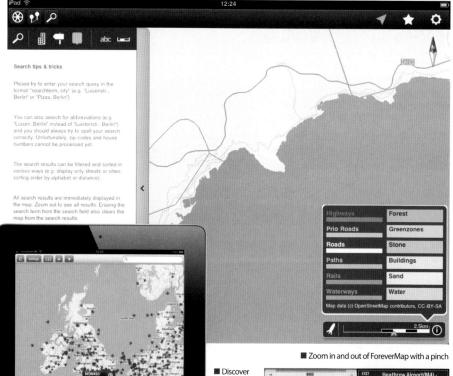

■ Zoom in and out of ForeverMap with a pinch

■ Discover
what's in the
sky above
your head
with the
Plane Finder
HD app…

■ In the 3D
view CoPilot
shows you
which turn
to take to get
home safely

News

If you're hungry for the latest news then the iPad is the perfect gadget to sate your appetite. We all have different interests when it comes to news, so there are specialist apps for every genre of news – like the world of science fiction for example. Most newspapers have an online edition, but that can be a fiddle to navigate using your iPad's Safari browser. We'll take a look at a couple of the best iPad newspaper apps to help you enjoy a decent digital version of your favourite newspaper without having to pinch to zoom in on small web browser text. There are even apps that will turn your iPad into a newsreader, so you can listen to headlines from any news source you choose while on the move. There's even an app that enables you to stream your favourite podcasts straight to your iPad without you having to download and sync them. The iPad offers so much in the way of news, you're guaranteed to stay informed.

"There are specialist apps for every genre of news"

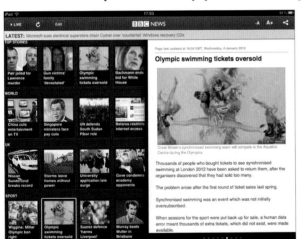

■ News is broken up into helpful headlines that you can explore in a tap

■ The BBC News app lets you watch events however you want

■ The New York Times Newsstand app is perfectly formatted for iPad

■ Browse through topics via category or search for something in the Guardian

■ The Guardian Newsstand app is well presented and ideal for iPad use

5 essential apps

01 The Guardian
Price: Free **Developer:** Guardian News and Media Limited

 This is the digital edition of the popular *Guardian* newspaper. Although the app is free to download you'll need to pay £3.99 for a 12-month subscription. Headlines are grouped under sections like Top stories or World news. All the stories are cross-referenced, making it easy to discover more information about an event. If you've a Wi-Fi connection there are video clips and podcasts to stream. There's a customisable dock where you can store links to your favourite features.

02 BBC News
Price: Free **Developer: Media Applications**

 Through this app you can get all the latest breaking news from the BBC and its global network of journalists delivered in an attractive and engaging interface. Stories are arranged in categories, including Top Stories, UK News and World News and cover a wide range of topics, including world news, politics, technology and sport. The app also offers the BBC News Channel streamed live, plus social features.

03 Sky News
Price: Free **Developer:** BSkyB

A well-presented and easily accessible app that places all the latest breaking news into your hands and allows you to decide what you want to watch and how you want to watch it. Includes live feeds and in-depth reports and analysis, plus a timeline that allows you to follow the day's events and unravel key moments in the past 24 hours. The best feature is the ability to rewind news feeds so you never miss a story.

04 Blastr
Price: Free **Developer:** NBC Universal, Inc.

If you're a science-fiction fan then Blastr is a useful way to beam stories and images from a variety of SF genres straight to your iPad. You can browse for stories via Sections like Horror or Rumors, or scroll through the latest news in chronological order. Just watch out for those spoilers.

05 NYTimes
Price: Free **Developer:** The New York Times Company

The New York Times app is free to download, but you'll need to subscribe to enjoy its rich in-depth content. Like the Guardian app you can tap on a section to add it to your Favorites, change the font size and enjoy photos and video clips.

5 essential apps

01 Aelios Weather

Price: £2.99/$4.99
Developer: Jime

 If you are the sort of person who travels around a lot then this is a lavishly-produced app to help you track the weather all over the planet. You can jump to any country by moving and pinching maps, get 24-hour forecasts that update regularly and seven-day forecasts to help you plan ahead. It also looks fantastic, which doesn't harm its appeal at all. Perfect.

02 Weather HD

Price: £0.69/$0.99
Developer: vimov, LLC

 This app isn't as informative as some of the others, but it's the prettiest to look at. The current weather conditions are represented using colourful HD videos. Clouds float by, raindrops fall or the Sun rises over windblown wheat stalks. This enables the app to function as attractive moving wallpaper. There's also text to inform you of temperature, humidity and wind strength.

03 Aero Weather Pro

Price: £2.49/$3.99
Developer: Pascal Dreer

 Thanks to AeroWeather Pro you can get current and precise weather conditions, as well as forecasts, which are used by pilots for their flight preparations. You can choose worldwide airport weather stations from the built-in database by either name of ICAO code and data will be shown in its original format or fully decoded into easy-to-understand texts.

04 Moon Calendar

Price: £0.69/$0.99
Developer: Rivolu Pte Ltd

 This app lets you understand and track the movements of our moon. It provides plenty of lunar insight including when you can expect new moons, full moons or even find out when the sun will rise in your location. Everything is presented in a great-looking interface and it's easy to use, making this the perfect app for lunar gazers everywhere.

05 Weather+

Price: £0.69/$0.99
Developer: International Travel Weather Calculator

 If you need a weather forecast in a hurry then this app places all you need to know on a single screen. Various widgets give you time, temperature, humidity and wind strength. You can customise the screen to simplify it, so only the most useful information is visible against the background.

Weather

Most of us will just want an app that forecasts the weather in our area for the next few days – and there are plenty of apps that perform that function very well.

We have trawled through the App Store for apps that will bring you a wide range of weather-related information. There's a deluge of weather-centric apps to choose from, which can make it a challenge to find which apps are essential (and which actually work!). When choosing our five essential apps we have gone for variety, to make sure that all your weather-related needs will be covered. You'll then know when to reach for the umbrella or a tube of suntan lotion.

We've gone for apps that display the forecasts as attractive weather-themed videos, apps that display satellite cloud maps plus apps that give you more specialist forecasts like pollen counts. Ultimately, we suspect that you'll only ever need one decent weather app, but here are five anyway!

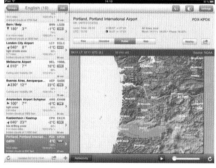
■ Get sleek and stylish updates with Aero Weather…

■ Aelios Weather draws its information from a wealth of trusted sources for you to get the best weather insight as you can

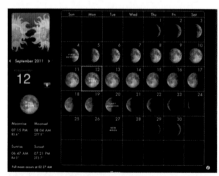
■ Monitor the movements of the moon with the aptly named Moon Calendar app

■ Aelios Weather present the weather where you are in a sleek and stylish manner

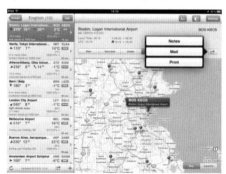
■ Aero Weather makes it easy to share your current climate with other people.

Photography

Thanks to your ever-present iPad 2 there's no danger that you'll miss a photo (or video) opportunity. The built-in Camera app enables you to focus on your subject matter and capture a decent exposure much of the time, but there will be occasions when you may want to produce more creative-looking results. Some of our essential apps enable you to turn photos into striking works of art or paintings at the touch of a button, so you can impress your friends with your apparent artistic skills. Another of our essential apps gives you a wide range of filters to play around with, turning ordinary snapshots into extraordinary retro images with attractive borders, amongst many other fancy effects. There's even an app to compliment and improve your Photoshop productivity while on the move. If you're into photography then you'll find thousands of products on the App Store to help you unleash your inner creativity and produce stunning photos that you'll want to show off.

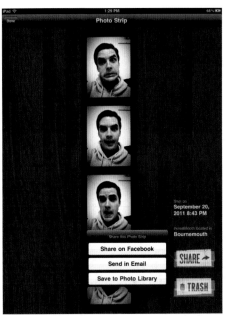
■ You can easily share IncrediBooth's results

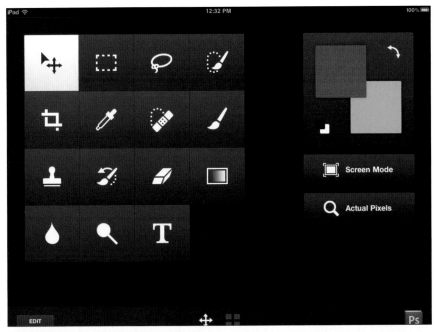
■ Adobe Nav is an excellent tool to use to edit your images while on the move

■ Create stunning images with Filterstorm

5 essential apps

01 Photogene for iPad
Price: £1.99/$2.99
Developer: Omer Shoor

 Photogene is a photo-editing app that is packed full of fun features to make the process enthralling rather than a chore. Included in the package are tools to help you crop and straighten images, adjust the colours, reduce red-eye and apply special effects such as reflection and vignette. You can also get arty on your pictures by applying filters, text boxes and frames.

02 Filterstorm
Price: £2.49/$3.99
Developer: Tai Shimizu

 Using a uniquely crafted touch interface, Filterstorm allows for more intuitive editing than its desktop counterparts with a toolset designed for serious photography. Ideal for photography professionals or any who wants to get the most out of their pictures, this app presents a varied toolset and allows you to create and apply artistic brilliance.

03 Strip Designer
Price: £1.99/$2.99
Developer: Jens Egeblad

 This app, as the name somewhat suggests, allows you to turn your photographs into comic strips. By selecting one of the many included templates you simply import your images and style them up by cropping, angling and applying speech bubbles and captions. It's great fun and will help you craft and tell stories through photos.

04 Adobe Nav for Photoshop
Price: £1.49/$2.99
Developer: Adobe Systems

 This companion app provides a whole new way to interact with Photoshop CS5 on your computer. Transfer images from you iPad directly to Photoshop and use it to select and browse through open Photoshop documents while on the move. This, along with other Adobe apps such as Eazel and Color Lava make mobile artwork easy,

05 IncrediBooth
Price: £0.69/$0.99
Developer: Synthetic Infatuation

 Featuring same dynamics as the versatile Hipstamatic app, Incredibooth lets you take amazing photo strips anywhere using the cameras of you iPad. The app comes packed with themes that you can instantly apply to your images plus options to share the whole strip.

Essential apps

5 essential apps

01 2Do
Price: £4.99/$6.99 **Developer:** Guided Ways Technologies Ltd

One way to keep organised is to write a list and cross tasks out as they're done. Unlike some free apps, 2Do enables you to group various tasks into different calendars. You can also prioritise tasks so that the most urgent ones are at the top. You can even assign notes and pictures and add practical actions that let you call or mail a contact in a click. Add an alarm and you'll receive a notification when it needs to be done.

02 Dropbox
Price: Free **Developer:** Dropbox

There are plenty of file-sharing apps, but Dropbox stands out from the crowd. The free service gives you a Dropbox folder on your computer and one on your iPad. When you drag a file into your computer's Dropbox it's automatically uploaded to an online folder, enabling you to view the file using the iPad. You can pay to increase the 2GB storage capacity. A fast and effective file-sharing app.

03 Keynote
Price: £6.99/$9.99 **Developer:** Apple

Keynote is a powerful presentation tool that has been on the Mac for a while, but with this iPad edition you can carry on working while on the move, now by syncing with iCloud too. Cleverly using the iPad's touch interface, the app allows you to choose from templates, create sophisticated animations and much more. Well worth a purchase.

04 Pages
Price: £6.99/$9.99 **Developer:** Apple, Inc

Anyone unsure of ditching their laptop in favour of an iPad need only look at Pages. This app is a versatile desktop publishing app that lets you create professional-looking page designs in minutes. With an intuitive set of tools, plenty of tutorials and templates, you can instantly create eye-catching letters, reports, flyers, cards, posters and more and customise them easily.

05 Pocket Informant HD
Price: £0.59/$0.99 **Developer:** Apple

This is an integrated calendaring and GTD-based tasks solution app that allows you to log in any details you want and track them easily. Navigating through the calendar feels natural – you simply swipe or tap the calendar on the left page – and you can assign icons to individual events or tasks.

■ Create your own posters, fliers, brochures… pretty much whatever you want in the brilliant Pages app

Productivity

Thanks to apps, your iPad can be many things. It has the power to become a communications device, a camera or even a games console. It can also help you get things done in the home or in your office thanks to a range of essential Productivity apps. In this section we'll show you apps that enable you to access (and even share) important documents while you're out of the office, so you're no longer chained to your desk. If you're a MobileMe user then you can access your iDisk from your iPad too even use your device to create wonderfully stylish pages and documents that will really command attention. Of course, we couldn't fail to include some quality personal organiser apps – mainly because there are just so many on the App Store that they're almost impossible to overlook. Here's a run down of those essential productivity apps to get your iPad working for you.

Learn more about Pages

Scroll through the document. Touch the images and text. And experience the most powerful word processor ever made for a mobile device.

■ With Dropbox you can transfer files with an incredible amount of ease

■ The Pages app on the iPad is a great tool that lets you create a variety of things while on the move

Reference

We all take the internet for granted as a source of information, and the iPad is often the portal we use when we need to access the world wide web's ocean of knowledge. Although the Safari app's Google search field is often our first port of call looking for information, it can take a while to wade through hundreds of results before we find what we're after. The apps featured in this section should help you narrow down your search to find relevant information more quickly, whether it's crime statistics for your hometown or the missing link in your family tree. We've also included the obligatory augmented reality app, so that you can discover what's out there in the universe above our heads through the iPad 2's camera! Our essential reference apps should help you filter your search for information more effectively.

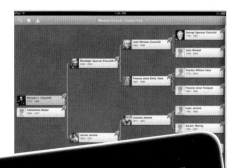
■ Browse your family trees while on the move in Ancestry

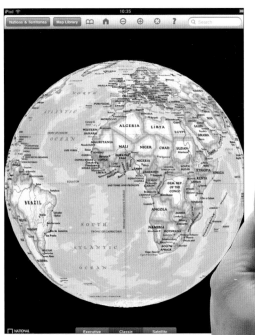
■ Play with the globe in World Atlas HD

■ Explore our planet with World Atlas HD's map

5 essential apps

01 World Atlas HD
Price: £1.49/$1.99

Developer: acrossair

 Designed specifically for iPad, National Geographic's new and improved World Atlas HD app puts the best, most detailed maps into the palm of your hand. You can jump to anywhere in the world instantly and grab all kinds of facts and insight about the countries you tap on. You can also learn all abut the flags and cultures.

02 Airports
Price: £2.99/$4.99

Developer: Peter Lundkvist

 This is an insightful and enthralling app for anyone interested in aviation. A quick search function lets you find airports by city, name, ICAO or IATA code and the app comes bulging with a wide range of data, including the dimensions and surface type of each runway, time zone, sunrise/sunset times and ATIS frequencies. The perfect app for plane spotters.

03 The Night Sky
Price: £0.69/$0.99

Developer: iCandi Apps

 This app enables you to see the stars, planets and satellites just by standing there and holding your device up to the night sky. All names of the stars and other objects will then be presented on your screen in real-time. It's a truly magical app that is great for showing off your device to friends and engaging and enthralling children keen to learn about the stars.

04 Wikipanion Plus for iPad
Price: £2.99/$4.99

Developer: Robert Chin

Accessing Wikipedia has never been faster and easier thanks to this app. It provides the complete Wiki database in one handy app that is quicker to access than via the web and comes packed with features. So if you're struggling in that next pub quiz, whip this out and get a wealth of worldly information at your fingertips.

05 Ancestry
Price: Free

Developer: Ancestry.com

 If you're investigating your family tree then chances are you'll be a member of Ancestry.com. This app formats that site for your iPad, enabling you to view or edit trees with ease and even upload photos of family heirlooms. This well-designed app provides an easy way to share family trees with relatives.

Social networking

Many of us spend more time socialising online than we do in the flesh, enabling us to sustain friendships with family, friends and colleagues over any distance. Your ever-present iPad is a key tool in helping you keep up-to-date with your online friends. We'll take a look at apps that let you find out who's doing what, and discover apps to communicate, free of charge, with other iPad users. If you use any of the main social networking sites then you'll find dedicated apps that let you access these sites with ease. We'll take a look at the apps from big-hitters like Facebook and Twitter, and show you ways to gather different networks into a single app. As well as keeping up with the social whirl we'll also show you an app that allow you to add even more personality to your tweets too.

■ Twitter has now been integrated in iOS 5 to make it easier than ever to tweet away

■ After a long wait, Facebook now has its own dedicated iPad app

■ Stay in your social loop with ease thanks to the intuitive IM+ app

■ With the Facebook app it is now even easier to stay in touch with friends and share your photos

5 essential apps

01 Coachpad
Price: £2.99/$4.99
Developer: Andrew Empson

This app is a brilliant teaching tool to help you design custom training drills, manage your team and record data. It caters from a wide range of sports, including football, tennis, hockey and basketball and is very easy to use – if you want to create a new training exercise then you just drag the equipment onto the playing surface and add in whatever elements you want.

02 Bike Repair HD
Price: £2.49/$3.99
Developer: Atomic Softwares

Cycling can be a great way to stay fit, but if you have mechanical problems it can be expensive. Buying this app could save you a bob or two as it shows you how to diagnose and fix common faults. Solve a problem by tapping on the appropriate part. Scroll through the list of possible problems and see an illustrated step-by-step guide on how to fix the fault.

03 Sky Sports News
Price: Free
Developer: BSkyB

This sleek, well-designed app is rammed with content – from insight and opinion to all the latest scores, behind the scenes news and sports results. An essential download for any self-confessed sports freak, it is a great, stylish way to get all the latest sports news in a format that is easy to navigate and digest on your iPad. Another great app from Sky, then…

04 Golfshot: Golf GPS
Price: £20.99/$29.99
Developer: Shotzoom Soft

You will need a 3G iPad to get the most out of this app, but it features a handy GPS rangefinder with distances to the front, center and back of the green, up to 40 professionally-mapped targets per hole and much more. So if you want to navigate your way around the course and ensure that you never lose your ball, then this is the perfect app for you.

05 NHL GameCenter 2011-2012 Premium
Price: Free
Developer: NHL Interactive

If you're into hockey then this app comes packed with scores, stats, photos and more. If you upgrade to the Premium edition in-app then you also get access to a live game radio, video highlights and picks of the week. Perfect for the armchair fan, we wish more sports had this.

Sports

There are many sports and recreational activities to enjoy, so no matter what sport you're interested in, there's bound to be an app for you in our sporting must haves. We have an app that enables cyclists to save repair bills by diagnosing mechanical problems and showing them the solutions. If you're aspiring to be the next 'Special One' then there are loads of decent coaching apps available that cater for a wide range of sports, including CoachPad, that makes creating your own training exercises a breeze. We have also picked out the best app for up-to-the-minute sports news, a useful app for improving your golf and we take a look at the ultimate app for the armchair ice hockey fan, which is so good that we wish other sports would follow suit and emulate the format. So, as you can see, the wonderful world of sport is well served on iPad.

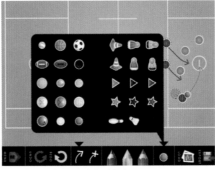

■ Teaching made easy with CoachPad

■ Get up-to-the-minute sports updates thanks to Sky Sports News

■ Everything you need to know about ice hockey in one lush app

■ The Sky Sports News app has videos you can watch while on the move

Essential apps

■ Word Lens is a genius app that can help with translations really quickly

■ Use Wikihood to get a wealth of information on local areas

Travel

Your iPad is the perfect travel companion, especially when packed with our selection of essential Travel apps. There are apps for every stage of your trip. Before you go, use apps to read hotel reviews from fellow travellers before making a hotel booking, or plan which places to visit when abroad by following other's recommendations. Use apps to search for the best travel deals (whether flight or car hire) and make a booking directly from your iPad. If you're planning to travel by plane we have an app to let you check out all the latest flight details. If you're staying at home you can use an app to take a tour of local points of interest and learn about your town's history. There's even an app that turns your iPad 2's camera into a foreign text translator (though it is limited to dealing with short signs that have nice clean fonts). And it all takes up a lot less space than an A-Z and a bumper English/French phrasebook!

■ Kayak HD allows you to find cheap hotels and flights easily

■ Read reviews and then find places of interest on a map with Trip Advisor

Utilities

Thanks to the App Store's Utilities category you can turn your iPad into the type of gadget that James Bond would be proud to own (although he'd probably trash it before the end of the movie!). There are Utility apps that enable you to pinpoint your iPad's location on a map and even wipe its precious data if it falls into enemy hands. If your iPad is stolen then there are secure data storage apps that will keep your passwords and bank details safe from prying eyes. If you regularly access websites that use Flash content then there is a web browser that can suit your needs. And there are many more brilliant apps available on the App Store that perform thousands of other cool functions – so make sure you have a browse through them and you're sure to find plenty of apps with a license to thrill.

"There are apps that perform thousands of cool functions"

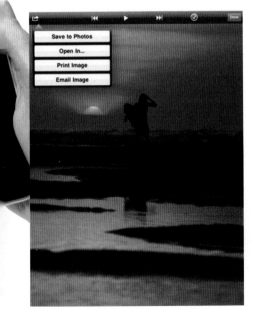

■ Watch Flash content on your iPad with the brilliant Skyfire Web Browser app…

■ FileBrowser allows you to transfer files between devices with ease

5 essential apps

01 Find My iPhone
Price: Free **Developer:** Apple

If you only download one app from the Utility category then make sure that it's this one. It could save you lots of time, stress and expense (though you'll need to make sure that the Find My iPad option is turned on in the Settings>iCloudmenu). If you lose your iPad, download the Find My iPhone software onto your Mac or iPhone. It'll pin-point your device's location on a map.

02 1Pssword Pro
Price: £10.49/$14.99 **Developer:** Agile Web Solutions

If you find it hard to remember multiple passwords then the 1Password Pro app will help. This enables you to store passwords for accounts like bank, MobileMe or iTunes safely. It'll even log you into your password-protected websites with a tap. It may be a relatively pricey app, but if someone gets their hands on your financial data then it could cost you a lot more.

03 Skyfire Web Browser for iPad
Price: £2.99/$4.99 **Developer:** Skyfire Labs, Inc

This web browsing app has always been a popular replacement for Safari and featured tabbed browsing months prior to the iOS 5 release. The best thing about this app is that it is an iPad web browser that actually lets you watch Flash content and has now undergone a few iOS 5 enhancements of its own, including the option to switch to desktop content in an instant.

04 PDF Reader – iPad Edition
Price: £2.99/$4.99 **Developer:** Kdan Mobile Soft

This sophisticated and easy to operate app gives you the ability to read just about anything, including Microsoft Office files, image files and even audio files. A great app to have around for times of need. And there will be many.

05 FileBrowser
Price: £2.99/$4.99 **Developer:** Stratospherix

Having this app installed on your device is akin to having Windows Explorer or Mac Finder on your iPad that allows you to access network folders on Macs, Windows, Linux and NAS drives. You can stream movies and music over Wi-Fi at home, access servers at work and work remotely with confidence that all of your files can be transferred around without any problems. For the price you pay, this is rammed full of features.

Your problems solved

If you have trouble with any aspect of using your iPad then you've come to the right place. Pull up a seat and let's sort it out

Can't connect to Wi-Fi

I can't seem to be able to connect my iPad to my home Wi-Fi signal or ones at hot spots in cafes and places like that. Is my iPad broken?

A There are lots of reasons why the iPad can't pick up a signal or connect to a Wi-Fi service, but some of those are outside the remit of this magazine as they are highly technical. The simpler solutions are that firstly, Wi-Fi might be turned off. Tap on the Settings app and tap on 'Wi-Fi'. If it is turned off then there is a slider to move to turn it back on. The next reason is that the iPad might be able to find the Wi-Fi network, but if it is secured – and your home network should be – then you will need to enter the network key (the password) for it. Firstly, select the right network from the ones listed under 'Choose a Network…' Tap on it. If it requires a network key it will immediately ask you for it. This is the password that your home network uses. Type it

in exactly and it should now connect. Cafes that have free Wi-Fi still often use passwords, but the process can be slightly different. Follow the same procedure by going to Wi-Fi and selecting the network you want. You will now join the network. If it's completely unrestricted, that will be all you have to do. If it requires a password then normally this is accessed through a web browser. It should automatically load Safari and take you to the homepage where the password can be entered. If it doesn't, then try tapping on Safari and running it yourself.

The other reasons for lack of Wi-Fi connectivity can simply be that you are too far away from the signal or that the signal is being interfered with by other equipment. If you have a wireless handset phone located next to the Wi-Fi router, for example, it can interfere with it. Try moving it or the router somewhere else to see if it will work there.

■ If you are having problems connecting to a Wi-Fi network, check to make sure that it is actually there!

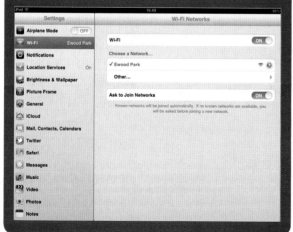

Recharging via USB

I've plugged my iPad into the USB lead and connected it to my computer, but it never seems to charge. Unlike, for example, if I plug my iPhone into it.

A The simple answer is that no, it might not do. The charge available through USB isn't high and the iPad demands a lot of juice to recharge. That's why the iPad comes with a mains charger. For fast recharging, you should use that instead. When the iPad is connected to a computer it can recharge, but not usually if the iPad is on, or even if it is in standby and you have a lot apps running that use notifications, because they will still secretly check for alerts. To give your iPad the best chance to recharge through the USB lead, either make sure that no apps are running and none are in suspend mode through multitasking. See the question further on about multitasking. To give your iPad the best chance of recharging, turn it off completely – see the next question.

Turning the iPad off

Normally I just press the little black button at the top of the iPad to turn it off, but I notice that the battery has

gone down slightly the next time I turn it on again. A friend of mine said that it was just in standby mode and not actually turned off, so how do I really turn it off?

A The beauty of the iPad is that you can put it into standby mode and it uses very little power. When you want to use it, one press of a button instantly brings it on. However, it does still use some power when in standby mode, especially if you have lots of apps multitasking.

To turn your iPad off completely, press and hold down the on/off button on the top right until the screen goes black and a red bar with the words "Slide to power off" appears. Slide the bar across to power down the iPad or tap Cancel to go back. When you turn it on again it will take approximately 30 seconds to power back up. Incidentally, the button on the top is called both the on/off button and also the sleep/wake button, depending on which action you are actually doing.

Charging the iPad

I am using the power charger for the iPad but it takes ages for it to recharge. Is there any way of speeding the process up?

■ If you have lots of apps running at the same time, then charging via the USB lead is nigh on impossible

| iPad 📶 | | 12:09 | | 54% 🔋 |

| Documents | Undo | **Term Paper** | ℹ 🖼 🔧 ⤢ |

Lullworth Co...

Aute duisim zzriusto elit illut ni...

⬅ Share and Print

✉ **Email Document**

🖨 **Print** ＞

Share via iWork.com

🎵 **Send to iTunes**

☁ **Copy to iDisk**

Copy to WebDAV

■ With the new version of the operating system you now have more ways to export your work documents

"It's very rare for the iPad to completely freeze, but it can still happen"

A *Normally, the mains power charger will recharge the iPad fairly quickly, but if it's taking a long time it's probably because you have a lot of applications running at once. So the solution is just the same as if recharging using the USB lead. If you ensure that no applications are running in the background then it should recharge pretty quickly, even on standby mode. If you turn the iPad off completely, however, it will recharge very quickly.*

Frozen iPad

My iPad has completely locked up. The Home button and the on/off button don't do anything and the screen is frozen and unresponsive. Please help!

A *The iPad may run a mobile operating system but it's still a computer and computers do occasionally crash. It's very rare for the iPad to completely freeze, but it can still happen. In this case press the Home button and the on/off button together for 10 seconds. The iPad should then reset itself.*

3G problems

I have recently bought an iPad secondhand that has 3G mode built in but I can't seem to get it to work, whatever I do! Is there anything I should be doing with the iPad to activate it?

A *There are two things about the 3G reception. The first is that your iPad needs to have a microSim installed that allows for a data package to be paid for. Without one, you can't access the 3G network. Numerous mobile network vendors offer packages based on how much information you access over the 3G network and bill you every month. So, you need the microSim and a data plan package.*

The other thing is that reception can be variable depending on where you are, so some more remote areas of the country don't have any 3G coverage at all, while others are rated only for reception outside buildings, not indoors. It's worth checking the coverage maps by each vendor to make sure the areas important to you are fully covered so you can fully enjoy 3G out and about.

Exporting documents

I use Pages and Numbers a lot, but it's a bit of pain to export documents through iTunes all the time. What else can I do to export them?

A *If you go back out of a document to the general documents view there are options to email the document, share via iWork.com or use cloud storage services like iDisk or a specific web server using WebDAV. If you are running iOS 5 (and have the latest versions of the apps installed on your device) then you can also sync documents wirelessly to your iCloud and they will be automatically updated on your other devices, such as your iPhone or Mac.*

Unresponsive screen

My iPad was working just fine, but recently the screen became unresponsive and sometimes things slow right down and then speed right up again making it pretty much unusable really. What do you think is causing this to happen and how do I fix it?

A *Try resetting the iPad (see the 'Frozen iPad' question). If that doesn't fix the problem then it's likely to be a hardware fault. Take the iPad into your nearest Apple store and if it's under warranty then you exchange it.*

TOP TIPS

Take a screenshot

If you want to take a screenshot of whatever is on the screen at that moment, press the on/off button and the Home button at the same time. The screen grab will be saved in your Photos folder under Saved Photos. It can be emailed, printed, tweeter and more.

Delete apps

Tap and hold on an icon for any app until all the apps start to wobble. A cross also appears in the corner of each one. Tap this to call up the Delete dialogue box and then tap 'Delete'.

Delete emails

Delete old emails by swiping your finger over them from right to left. The word Delete will appear. Tap on this to remove it from your inbox.

Reorganise the Home screens

Tap and hold the icon for an app until the screen goes into wobble mode. Now, keep holding and move the icon around the screen. Release to drop into place.

Backing up forever

Whenever I come to back up my iPad by connecting it to iTunes through the computer, it seems to take an absolute age to do it. How can I make it do this much quicker?

A *If you are using an iPad 2 the answer may lie with the number of pictures you have on the camera roll, but it's more likely to be a dodgy app – there's no real reason with iOS 5 for it to be particularly slow.*

So, cancel the backup and, in iTunes, click on the entry for your iPad in the pane on the left side of the window. Now click on the Apps tab that appears above the central area of iTunes. There's an option to Sync Apps, which will have a tick in it. Click on this to remove the tick. Now try the backup. If it goes quickly then it was indeed a bad app. Now, put the tick back into Sync Apps but untick each app individually. Then, starting with the top one, put a tick in the first app and try the sync. If it works fine, put a tick into the next app and try again. Keep going through the apps until you get to one where the backup now takes forever. That's your bad app.

To fix the app, you should check to see if there is an update available for it. Click on Apps under the Library heading on the left side pane. On the bottom-right corner it will tell you if there are any updates for the app currently available. Click on this text or the right-facing arrow to go to the updates page. Is your app listed here? Even if it's not, we recommend that you keep all your apps updated anyway, so click on either Get Update for the individual app, or Download All to update everything.

Do another sync and, if it backs up properly, all is now fine. If it doesn't then it looks like the app is corrupt. Click on the Apps entry under Library again and then right-click on the app in question. From the dialogue box that appears, select 'Delete'. Remove the app from iTunes. Now, is the app working fine on the iPad itself? If so, then go ahead and sync and agree to the option that comes up to copy back to iTunes. This should put the good version of the app back into iTunes. If the app doesn't actually work on your iPad, then either delete it from the iPad first or, when doing the sync, decline the option to transfer back to iTunes as this will remove it from the iPad as well.

Hopefully your backing up should be much quicker now the corrupt app has been dealt with.

> ## "If the app doesn't work on your iPad, then either delete it from the iPad first or, when doing the sync, decline the option to transfer back to iTunes"

■ The key to finding bad apps is to untick Sync Apps and try them out one at a time

Feeling sleepy?

My iPad keeps turning itself off really quickly to the extent that I am perpetually having to switch it back on. This is really annoying because I do like to browse things while chatting and then I find that it's gone to sleep. Aside from coffee, how do you make it stay awake?

A *You either like the timed sleep mode or it gets on your nerves. Your iPad is set to go to sleep after two minutes of inactivity by default, but if you don't mind using power like there's no tomorrow go to the Settings app and tap on General. Tap on Auto-Lock and tap on 15 Minutes or Never. This will keep your device awake for longer.*

Multitasking woes

Some of my apps keep saying that my iPad's memory is running low and I should close other apps that are open. I know that multitasking is now supported but I don't know how the other apps are running or how to close them.

A *To see what apps are running under multitasking mode press the Home button twice, very quickly. The apps on the main screen fade and a panel will appear at the bottom of the screen showing the apps currently running. Tap and hold on any of them until they all start to wiggle and a red dash appears on the left corner of each icon. Tap the dash to close the apps so that the only one running is the one you are using.*

Syncing Outlook Mail, Calender and Contacts

I have Microsoft Outlook on my computer and want to be able to get my mail, contacts and calendars on my iPad. Can I do this and if so, how do I do it?

A *Plug your iPad in to the computer so that iTunes recognises it. Click on the name of your iPad under Devices in the left side panel. Then click on the Info tab above the main screen. There are entries for Sync Contacts, Sync Calendars and Sync Mail Accounts. Put a tick in each tickbox and ensure that Outlook is the program selected to sync with. Then click on Sync in the bottom-right corner. If you use iOS 5 and OS X 10.7.2 on your Mac then you can sync emails, contacts and calendars wirelessly using iCloud too.*

■ Tapping the Home button twice will bring up the apps that are currently multitasking

"Tap the dash to close the apps so that the only one running is the one you are using"

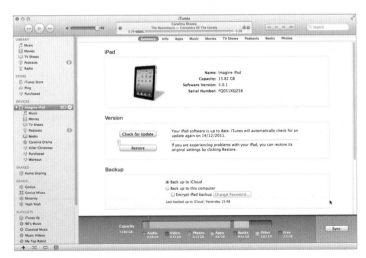

■ The ability to easily synchronise email, contacts and calendars with Outlook is a great feature of the iDevice

Not recognised

My iPad is no longer recognised by my computer. When I plug it in nothing appears under the Devices entry in iTunes. Please help, I'm afraid that my iPad may be broken!

A *Don't worry, the chances of your iPad being broken are very slim. Now there are some very technical causes for this kind of thing happening, but the two most common answers are that either the USB port you are plugging the iPad into is faulty or that iTunes has become corrupt. Try plugging the iPad into a different USB port. If that doesn't work, uninstall iTunes, download the latest version and re-install it. Then try it again. There's also a high chance that neither your computer nor your device are faulty. Instead, you may simply have a defective USB cable. If you have another lying around you should try connecting your iPad with that. If nothing works, you should try turning both iPad and computer off and on again; you'd be surprised how many problems that solves!*

TOP TIPS

Add a signature
Personalise your emails by adding a signature. Tap on Settings then go to Mail, Contacts, Calendars. Look down the list on the right for Signature. Tap this to enter your message.

Restrict your iPad
Go to the Settings app and tap on General and then on Restrictions. On the new page tap on Enable Restrictions, which requires a four-digit passcode to be set up.

Different fonts
If you use Notes to keep, well, notes, then check out the two additional fonts that you can use. Go to Settings, then Notes to select them.

Turn an iPad into a picture frame
Turn your iPad into a picture frame by going to Settings then Picture Frame. When you turn your iPad on, instead of swiping to unlock, tap on the Picture Frame icon.

Top ten tips for saving battery power

The iPad might be able to go all day, but the battery still runs out. Here's how to maximise what power you have

01 Turn your iPad off at night

Not standby, but actually off. You aren't using it but the apps can be so shut it down. Hold down the on/off button until prompted.

02 Turn off Wi-Fi

If you are not using the internet and don't anticipate doing so then turn the Wi-Fi signal off. Tap on Settings and slide Airplane mode to on to turn off all wireless functions.

03 Turn down brightness

How bright the display is affects power usage. The brighter it is, the more power it uses. Tap on the Settings app and then tap on Brightness & Wallpaper. There's a slider that sets how bright the display is. Tap and hold then slide to the left to reduce it.

04 Location services

The iPad has something called 'Location Services' that enables apps to discover where you are. They use the Wi-Fi or 3G signal to do this, which uses power. If you want to squeeze a bit more power out of the battery, turn this feature off by going to the Settings app and tapping on General. Tap on Location Services and either toggle individual apps off or turn the entire service off.

05 Push and Fetch

These are two services that your Mail, Contacts and Calendars use. If you allow the apps to keep checking for new mail or information

they can use up battery power. Push is where new information, such as new email, is sent from the server to your iPad, so your device gets it as soon as it is on the system. It's certainly useful if you really need it, but it drains the battery. So, in Settings, tap on Mail, Contacts, Calendars and tap again on Fetch New Data. There is an entry for Push, so use the slider to set it to Off.

06 Push off

As explained, Fetch is a scheduled service where the iPad goes to the server and checks to see if there is any mail. This can be as often as every 15 minutes. Now, if you are using Push you don't need Fetch, so tap on Manual. Also, if you've set Push to Off, to save battery power set Fetch to Manual as well. Now nothing will be checked unless you run those apps and manually check for new info.

> "Slide Airplane mode to on to turn off all wireless functions"

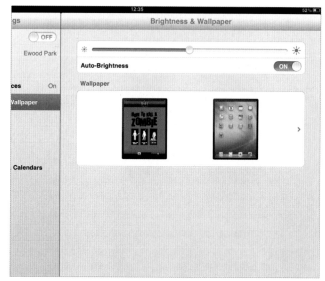

■ The brightness of the screen affects how much power the iPad uses. Turn it down to make the battery last longer

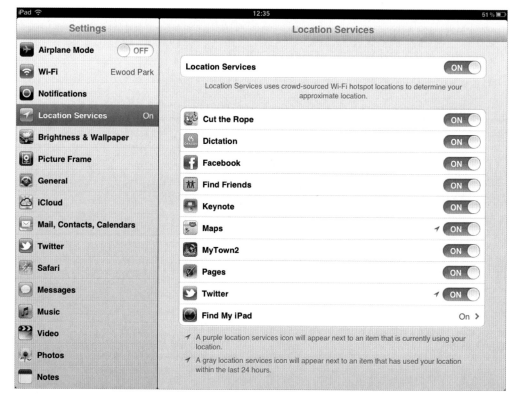

■ While a valuable service to use, you may not want all your apps to be constantly demanding to know where you are

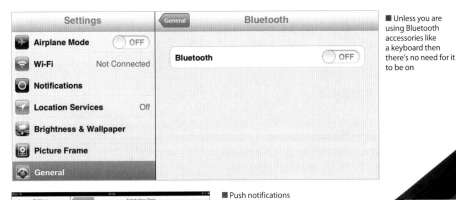

■ Unless you are using Bluetooth accessories like a keyboard then there's no need for it to be on

■ Push notifications send mail and other information from the server when it arrives. Turn it off and check manually when needed

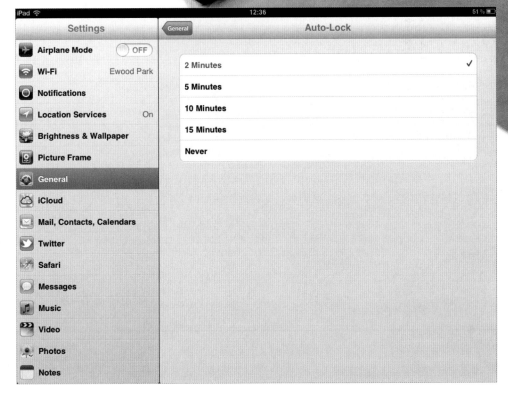

"If you aren't using the iPad but it's still on, it's using up valuable power"

07 Sleep

Let your iPad go into sleep mode more quickly. If you aren't using the iPad but it's still on, then it's using up valuable power needlessly. Let it go into sleep mode more quickly by tapping firstly on Settings then on General. Tap on Auto-Lock and change the time to 2 minutes. If you value your battery life, we recommend you don't have it set to 'Never'.

08 Don't multitask

Don't leave any apps running in multitask mode. Close down the ones that you aren't using. It may take a little bit of getting used to, but your battery life will drastically improve. See the earlier question called 'Multitasking woes' for more details.

09 No Bluetooth unless necessary

Unless you have to use connected external devices like a keyboard, there is no need for Bluetooth to be turned on; having it on with nothing connected still wastes battery life. Go into Settings and tap on Bluetooth, then slide the switch so that it's off.

10 Keep out of the hot and cold

Surprisingly, extremes of temperature will significantly affect your iPad's battery life and performance. Don't leave your device in the car overnight or on a table in the sun.

■ The time it takes before your iPad goes into sleep mode can be adjusted so that it happens more quickly

Helpdesk

Your iPad glossary

WHAT DOES IT ALL MEAN? WE GUIDE YOU THROUGH THE COMMON FEATURES AND TERMS THAT YOU'RE LIKELY TO ENCOUNTER WHILE USING YOUR iPAD

APPLE ID
This is the name and password you use to log into the various Apple services, such as iTunes, the App Store and iCloud.

APPLICATION (APP)
An application, or app, is a software program designed to perform one or more functions. Apps can be downloaded from the App Store.

APP STORE
The App Store is a digital distribution platform for Apple users. Users are able to browse, purchase and download iPad and iPhone apps from the App Store to run on their device.

■ You can shop and browse apps by popularity and category at the App Store.

DOCK
The Dock is a row of icons that can be set to appear at the bottom of your Home screen. The Dock is ever-present as you scroll through screens and allows you to access your favourite, most well-used apps easily. You can add and remove apps by pressing and holding on an icon until it starts to shake and then dragging it into position.

GAME CENTER
Apple's gaming portal where you can shop for new games, find friends and play against them online or compare high scores.

GESTURES
These refer to the finger commands that you perform on your iPad's touch screen to carry out various functions. With iOS 5, Multitasking Gestures have been added that let you use five fingers to pinch to reveal your Home screen or swipe up, left or right to reveal your multitasking bar or cycle between open apps.

GESTURES JARGON:
● **TAP**
This is the most common and basic gesture to perform on your iPad; it involves tapping the screen with your finger.

● **DOUBLE-TAP**
This involves tapping an object twice in succession. You use this gesture mainly for zooming or highlighting text.

● **TAP, HOLD & DRAG**
Some functions, such as highlighting text, copying and pasting require that you tap and hold down on the screen and then drag your finger to select what you want.

● **PINCH**
To zoom in or to open something, place your thumb and index finger, pinched together, on screen and spread them apart. To zoom out, perform the reverse.

● **SWIPE**
Swiping is one of your primary navigational tools. You perform a left or right swiping motion with your index finger to move through app pages or images in the Photos app, for instance.

HOME BUTTON
This is the large circular button on the front of your iPad that you use to quit apps and return to your iPad's Home screen.

HOME SCREEN
This is essentially the desktop of your iPad that you see when you boot up or unlock your device. From your Home screen you can launch apps and access your Settings.

iCLOUD
The iCloud is a free cloud storage and syncing service introduced as part of the iOS 5 update. With iCloud you can share data, files, music and photographs between devices without the need for manual connecting, syncing and transferring.

iCLOUD JARGON:
● **iTUNES IN THE CLOUD**
With iCloud, the music you purchase from iTunes appears automatically on all of your devices. You can also download past purchases where you want, when you want.

systems. The app boasts a wealth of new iOS 5 enhancements to make surfing the web a quick and easy experience.

SETTINGS
Accessible from the Dock or Home Screen, Settings is where you can tweak all aspects of your iPad and the apps and utilities that make it tick.

SIDE SWITCH
This is the small switch on the edge of the iPad that you can assign, via Settings, to act as a mute button or to lock your screen rotation.

SLEEP/WAKE BUTTON
This is the lozenge-shaped button on top of the iPad that you use to turn your device on and off.

WI-FI
Wi-Fi refers to a wireless networking system that allows you to connect to the internet without any cables. You will need access to a wireless router for this to work with your iPad.

● PHOTO STREAM
With iCloud, when you take a photo on one device, it automatically appears on all of your devices. Photos transferred from a digital camera connected to your Mac will also be pushed to your mobile devices.

● DOCUMENTS IN THE CLOUD
If you have the same iCloud-enabled apps on more than one device, iCloud automatically keeps your documents up to date across all devices.

iOS
Whereas Macs run on an operating system called Mac OS X, your mobile devices – iPhone, iPad and iPod touch – use iOS. The latest version is iOS 5 and you will need this installed to enjoy the benefits of iCloud.

iTUNES
This is Apple's flagship digital distribution centre that lets users browse, purchase and download a wide range of digital media, including music, books, movies and TV shows. Using an Apple ID, users log in and store payment details to make downloading media quick and easy.

iTUNES JARGON:
● FEATURED
All of the latest, most notable music, movies and TV shows will be showcased under this tab at the front of their respective store windows.

● TOP CHARTS
See what's hot and popular on the iTunes Store by tapping on this tab.

■ iTunes is the ultimate digital marketplace for buying and downloading new music and entertainment through your iPad.

● GENIUS
This is a feature that recommends new music, films and shows based on what is currently in your library. Genius can also create playlists for you.

● iTUNES U
iTunes is also a great source of educational materials, and you'll find a wide range of digital books, videos and podcasts by clicking on the 'iTunes U' link.

● REDEEM
Occasionally you may be gifted a product from iTunes in the form of a code. Click on the 'Redeem' link and input the code to download the product.

NEWSSTAND
This app comes free with iOS 5 and is a place where all of your digital magazines and newspapers are stored and can be accessed.

SAFARI
This is Apple's premier web browsing app that comes as standard with all iPad operating

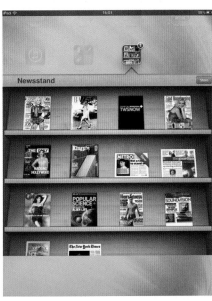

■ The Newsstand app is where all of your digital magazines and newspapers are safely stored.

Not just for dummies

New for OS X Lion

FREE

Mac for Beginners™
Everything you need to know to get started with your Apple Mac

- ✪ Setting up your Mac
- ✪ Get the most out of iTunes
- ✪ Learn about iPhoto & iMovie
- ✪ Master Safari, Mail and more

iPhone for Beginners™
Everything you need to know to get started with your iPhone

Over 350 tips for all iPhones

- ✪ Must-have apps
- ✪ Setting up your iPhone
- ✪ Essential guide to iTunes
- ✪ Troubleshooting tutorials

Android for Beginners™
All you need to get started with your Android device

- ✪ All the essential apps
- ✪ Setting up your device
- ✪ Learn about Gmail & Maps
- ✪ Full guide to Android Market

for Beginners

A clear, comprehensive series for people who want to start learning about iPhone, iPad, Mac, Android and Photoshop

Also in this series

Photoshop for Beginners

WordPress for Beginners

Bookazines
eBooks · Apps
www.imaginebookshop.co.uk

HIGH ST.
BUY IN STORE
High street

amazon
Kindle Store

ip
ImagineShop.co.uk

App Store